DEEPLY CANADIAN
New Submarines for a New Millennium

DEEPLY CANADIAN
New Submarines for a New Millennium

by

Julie H. Ferguson

BEACON PUBLISHING

Cover design by Tracey Palmer (photo with permission of BAE Systems)
Edited by Doris Fackler and Leslie Cholowsky
Printed and bound by Imprint Books

Care has been taken to trace the ownership of copyright material used in the text (including illustrations). The author and publisher welcome any information enabling them to rectify any reference or credit in subsequent editions.

Canadian Cataloguing in Publication Data

Ferguson, Julie H., 1945-
    Deeply Canadian

Includes bibliographical references
ISBN 0-9689857-0-X

1.Submarines (Ships)--Canada. 2. Canada. Canadian Armed Forces.
Canadian Submarine Service. I. Title

V859.C3F465 2001   359.9'3'0971   C2001-911508-3

Beacon Publishing
#5-300 Maude Road
Port Moody, BC
Canada V3H 2X6   http://www.beaconlit.com

Table of Contents

List of Illustrations:

List of Maps:

List of Tables:

Foreword
by
CAPTAIN (N) KEITH G. NESBIT, CD, (Retired)

We military people tend to be mesmerized by our machines. Thus, Canadian submariners have fretted for decades over the need to replace their three precious Oberon class undersea machines at the end of their useful lives. As Julie Ferguson so clearly shows in *Deeply Canadian*, machines have been only part of the story: at stake was the future of the Canadian Submarine Service itself. And during the years preceding the federal government's decision to acquire the new British-built *Victoria* Class, it often looked as if a major Canadian asset was "going down the tubes."

This situation was not new to the Canadian Navy. In 1970, the decision to scrap, without replacement, our invaluable and recently refitted aircraft carrier, *Bonaventure*, constituted the loss of much more than a machine. We bade farewell to our highly regarded Fleet Air Arm and, really, to naval aviation itself. This was an inestimable loss of a hard-won profession. Similarly, although of lesser consequence, the navy had previously given up its very credible minesweeping capability in deference to the higher priority being placed on destroyer-oriented anti-submarine warfare. Decades later, we found out how challenging it is to try and regain such a lost skill.

Ms. Ferguson's treatment of "The Great Canadian Submarine Debate" is classic. She has indeed done her homework and even those who were directly involved in the debate can learn from her analysis. Perhaps to many Canadians the "Great Debate" was over nuclear propulsion. And, while the ill-fated (and, to many, ill-conceived) objective of the 1987 defence White Paper to acquire nuclear attack submarines (SSNs) generated some much-needed public discussion about maritime responsibilities, the *real* question to be resolved was (or should have been) whether Canadian maritime defence capabilities should continue to include a sub-surface component in the post-Cold War era. Fortunately, thanks to astute and innovative naval leadership and some gutsy, strong support from some important fellow Canadians in places such as the Privy Council, common sense won. To the extent that public probing of high-level Government dealings would allow, Ms. Ferguson tells a great story.

That debate of the 1980's and 1990's has been of national benefit. There has been considerable maturing within the Canadian Forces, and it is likely that the navy's leadership has never been better. Today's admirals demonstrate a solid appreciation of how a multi-platform, multi-disciplinary team can be used to protect and further sovereign interests, which is the key to successful management of maritime affairs by a financially constrained "medium" nation having long coastlines. Moreover, those senior leaders have proven themselves highly adroit in matters of equipment acquisition. How the *Victoria* Class was funded makes for fascinating reading.

For the general reader, *Deeply Canadian* provides considerable insight into the Canadian Submarine Service itself. An admittedly paranoid cast of characters who have traditionally felt unappreciated by the rest of the navy, our submariners, like those of other nations, have an intensely professional approach to their job and an obvious "clan" mentality. This has been both a blessing and a curse. The inherently unsafe aspects of operating underwater dictate the need for a detailed knowledge by all crewmembers of all aspects of their underwater machine. The elitist feature simply derives from cramming a lot of bodies for a long time into a very confined space and demanding that they do a quite difficult job. Such clannishness must surely have been evident in our little World War II corvettes and minesweepers.

The reader may conclude that Canadians make ideal submariners. They have an ability to tolerate their fellow men, often under trying conditions. They have a dedicated, no-nonsense approach to their work. And they have a refreshingly irreverent (and somewhat less than 100% politically correct) sense of humour. Our submarine service may well be, in fact, the most *Canadian* part of the *Canadian* Forces.

In her previous book, *Through A Canadian Periscope*, Julie Ferguson provided a detailed account of the eighty-year history of the Canadian Submarine Service. In *Deeply Canadian*, her emphasis is upon the rationale for continuance of that service in the new millennium. She tells it like it is. Canada is a "medium maritime power" which has unique and unbelievably huge areas of responsibility off its shores. Credible caretaking requires a variety of tools: some armed, some not. The submarine is but one of the necessary tools. Responsibility for the effective use of sub-surface tools rests with the Canadian Submarine Service. And, as Ms. Ferguson describes so well, that service is now acquiring the precious machines that will enable them to do the job. Canada is staying in the underwater business.

Keith Nesbit

May 2000
Captain (N) Keith Nesbit, CD. (Ret.),
Former Commanding Officer, HMCS *Okanagan*,
Former Commander, First Canadian Submarine Squadron.

Preface

I was not alone in thinking that my last book, *Through a Canadian Periscope*, would turn out to be the eulogy of the Canadian Submarine Service--several highly placed naval officers thought so too. Happily we were proved wrong but it took awhile. The proposal to replace our three aging submarines with four British Upholder class boats was submitted to Mr. Chretien in the spring of 1996 following cabinet approval, but it did not receive his blessing until April 1998. The four used submarines are not enough but something, at least, to keep our navy operating in three dimensions--over, on, and under the sea.

I had planned to publish *Deeply Canadian* before the new submarine contract for the Upholder class submarines was signed, but personal considerations interfered with that timing. So instead of doing a selling job to help preserve the Canadian Submarine Service, *Deeply Canadian* is partly a sequel to *Through a Canadian Periscope*. My second book explains the reasons why Canada needs to continue operating submarines, details the long, drawn-out Upholder acquisition, and describes Canada's newest submarines for the non-naval reader. Like *Periscope*, it is not technical or minutely detailed but rather easy to read and, I hope, enjoyable. *Deeply Canadian* is also an exercise in public relations for the Canadian Submarine Service, a branch of our navy that is sadly not well known or well understood.

The excellent cooperation afforded me by the Department of National Defence and Maritime Command in Canada, as well as the Upholder Sales Team in the United Kingdom, does not mean that this book reflects their policies or opinions, nor does it mean that it is in any way official. *Deeply Canadian* is the work of an independent observer of the Canadian and international submarine scenes.

As always, the submarine community, both at home and abroad, afforded me respect and courtesy as I went about my task of gathering information, interviewing, and generally making a nuisance of myself. Without them this book could never have been written and, once again, I hope I have done justice to their trust in me.

Port Moody, B.C.   **Julie H. Ferguson**
May 2000   www.beaconlit.com

Acknowledgements

As writers gain more experience in both their subject areas and the mysteries of publishing, the size of the behind-the-scenes team decreases. Nonetheless, the volume of gratitude never diminishes--non-fiction writers are always in debt to those who provide them with information, illustrations, criticism, a bed, or a beer.

Although Dundurn Press Ltd. declined to publish this book, I must credit its publisher, Kirk Howard, for planting the seed for *Deeply Canadian* in 1996 and the Royal Navy's Flag Officer Submarines, Rear-Admiral Perowne, OBE, for watering it at a submariners' reunion in Victoria in May 1997, which he attended as the guest of honour. Later when I wanted to visit the Upholder submarines, Admiral Sir James Perowne and his secretary, Commander Malcolm Smith, RN, kindly arranged it for me.

In Canada, the navy was very generous in its time to help me better understand the importance of submarines to Canadian defence. Those involved have requested that they are not named, but they know who they are, and I will always remember their patience and hospitality.

On the British side of the pond, I was treated superbly as well. I have to thank Erith Davies of the Upholder Sales Team for giving me two days that any author would die for--submarine tours, presentations, specialists to interview, a gourmet dinner, and even a Sunday question-and-answer time in a country pub; Lieutenant Commander Peter Southern, RN, the Royal Navy Liaison Officer with the Upholder Sales Team for his delightful hospitality, good company, a tour of the Lake District, and invaluable assistance; the staff of GEC Marine--VSEL (now BAE Systems) in Barrow-in-Furness, both on and off the Upholders, who briefed me and allowed me to crawl all over HMS *Unseen* and the Shore Development Facility (Mike Smith, Keith Johnson, and David Wilton to name only three amongst many, and the company photographer); and the manager of the Majestic Hotel in Barrow who made my stay most comfortable and feel like a family affair.

Two individuals deserve a paragraph all to themselves. Captain (N) Keith Nesbit, CD (Ret) is a well-known Canadian submariner who has guided me before with generosity and humour. This time he has done much, much more. Keith provided all sorts of expert advice and material to further the project, as well as scrutinized the final manuscript. His incisive and insightful suggestions kept me on the straight and narrow and improved the book immeasurably. When he agreed to write the forward as well, I was delighted. Another gave beyond the call of duty: Commander Michael Young, CD, (Ret). Mike also put my manuscript through the wringer, making many excellent suggestions and correcting mistakes. Any that remain are mine.

There are many individuals who deserve recognition but were less directly involved in *Deeply Canadian:* Cdr. Lloyd Barnes (Ret), president of the Submariners' Association of Canada, Pacific branch, for the invitation that started this book rolling; Vice-Admiral Peter Cairns, (Ret) for his insight; Commodore Jan Drent (Ret) for his interest in my project and good ideas; Captain (N) Sherm Embree (Ret), for patiently unravelling AIP to a non-engineer; Rear-Admiral Ed Healey (Ret) for once again answering umpteen questions; Capt(N) Jay Plante (Ret) for his timely reminders; dozens of serving naval officers who must remain anonymous but were tireless in their assistance; the many members of SAOC, Pacific and Central branches; Sarah Trant and Lise Dessaint of the National Press Club; Dr. Jim McFarlane, president of International Submarine Engineering Ltd., for being there for me as always; Eileen Kernahan, my writing mentor; Elspeth Naismith for her company and encouragement when I am away from home; the staff of the Port Moody Public Library who are now resigned to finding "difficult to find" books for me; members of my book club for their support; the many submariners past and present for their undying interest in my projects; my dear friends, Stuart and Cathy Bennett, whose proximity to Heathrow means I use their spare room regularly but all too briefly; and my husband, James, for his patience.

Last but definitely not least, my two eagle-eyed editors deserve my heartfelt thanks. Gladys Fackler and Leslie Cholowsky, between them, have improved Deeply Canadian in many ways I could not see. Also I very much enjoyed working with Tracey Palmer who designed the striking cover for this book.

JHF

TO ALL THOSE WHO WORKED SO HARD TO ENSURE THAT THE CANADIAN SUBMARINE SERVICE SURVIVED BEYOND YEAR 2000.

Dolphin 72 B

Dive! Dive! Dive!

Mention the Snowbirds (with a capital S) to any Canadian and they immediately know that you are talking about the Canadian air force. As a nation we are very proud of our fighter aviation heritage that stems from WWI and our Snowbirds aerobatics team. Mention HMCS *Onondaga* and you are met with a blank stare. Sadly our underwater heritage, although the same age and just as distinguished, is virtually unknown. I suspect that if submarines performed at air shows from coast to coast and starred in movies, the Canadian Submarine Service would also have earned a place in every Canadian's heart. As it is, few Canadians know we have a submarine service; still fewer understand why we have one. Hopefully this book will change that.

At a time when many feel that Canada has little need of her armed services, the navy has acquired four submarines for the new millennium to replace the three old Oberon class boats. *Deeply Canadian* examines why Canada needs submarines at this time in the context of the current and predicted world order, our foreign and defence policies, and our maritime geography. What makes submarines so special, what kind of submarine we need, and whether the newly acquired Victoria class boats are suitable for the Canadian navy's requirements are discussed too. Along the way the book also takes brief looks at our submarine heritage, the traditional lack of enthusiasm for submarines in this country, and he unusual deal that the navy struck with the British Ministry of Defence to get the new submarines. *Deeply Canadian* does not make the argument to acquire submarines; it simply examines why we must keep our submarine force. It is an interesting story overall but it is often a disheartening one. The lack of visibility of our Canadian Submarine Service has meant that the submariners have had to fight for recognition and understanding from within the navy, successive governments, and the population as a whole. While they have made much progress, especially in the navy in the 1980s due to the enthusiasm of many non-submariners, they still haven't arrived--submarines are not and, probably never will be, the household name that the Snowbirds are.

I am not a submariner--merely a Canadian interested in defence matters in general and submarines in particular. I wrote this book because our submarine force needed more exposure and explanation as we move into a new era. *Deeply Canadian* is written by and for the average citizen in a way that avoids the buzzwords and jargon of defence matters and demystifies this specialized subject. It should be required reading for all our Members of Parliament.

I gathered much of the meat of the book from papers and articles written by experts that never reached the popular press and from documents obtained through Access to Information. In 1997 I spent ten days in Ottawa talking with those involved with the submarine replacement program and spent three days in England discussing the proposed offer with the Upholder Sales Team. I visited all four of the Upholders, now known as the Victoria class, spent hours on board HMS *Unseen*, and toured the shore development facility at Barrow-in-Furness.

The collapse of the Warsaw Pact scrambled the balance of power, sending us from a bi-polar world to a multi-polar one overnight. The world is now less predictable, with pockets of unrest, rising tensions, and conflict springing up in all sorts of unexpected places. In late 1996 the incumbent minister of national defence told Canadians that the Canadian Forces (CF) were facing more demands on their expertise than they had since the Korean War in the 1950s. Coming after the end of the Cold War, it was a sobering observation. In a time of severe defence cuts and a loss of 28,000 personnel, it was also worrying.

Much of the domestic demands have come from a shift in focus away from meeting NATO requirements to concentrating more on the protection of our sovereignty. At home the Oceans Act, a piece of federal legislation proclaimed in the late '90s, changed the way we manage our oceans and increased the navy's responsibilities in our vast holdings of maritime real estate. The number of serious encroachments on our ocean territory and resources has grown over the last decade and are unlikely to diminish.

Internationally the demands on the Canadian Forces have stemmed from the growth in the number of UN-style operations around the world in which Canada tends to participate. These have become more hazardous over the last ten years, putting Canadians in more danger than ever before. Our submarines have not participated abroad so far but that could change.

Canada's tiny force of three boats is a surprise to many that don't realize we operate submarines. It is also a surprise to those who know about submarines--they can't believe we have managed for thirty years with only three. Neither can they believe that all three are based on the Atlantic coast; we have not had a submarine presence in the Pacific for nearly twenty-five years. To set the size of the Canadian Submarine Service into perspective, other countries that operate less than six boats include Libya, Argentina, and the Netherlands, for example, and their maritime territories are vastly smaller than ours. By way of contrast, another small northern maritime country, Norway, operates twelve.

Here then are the arguments for the continuation of the Canadian Submarine Service.

Chapter One
CANADA'S SUBMARINE HERITAGE

Excellent though it is, Canada's submarine heritage is virtually unknown to the average Canadian. A good two-thirds of our population doesn't even know Canada owns and operates submarines. A few, when pressed, will explain about the boats at the West Edmonton Mall and then laugh apologetically. The truth is, in fact, very different. The Canadian Submarine Service is a national asset with decades of tradition, experience, and achievement--over eighty-five years worth. Should Canada lose this specialized branch and then need it again, experts estimate that it would take at least a generation to restore it--about twenty years--and an overwhelming amount of money.

The Canadian navy has had submarines on and off since 1914, only ten years short of the British Royal Navy and the United States Navy, who were pioneers. The rich and definitely unsung Canadian submarine tradition has been a boon to the navy but has been viewed by a few as a nuisance, sucking up the money for the surface ships and threatening to supersede them. Our submarine service ranks with the best in the world and, although it is small, it is a force to be reckoned with.

Why is it, then, that Canadians all know about our fighter pilots and not our submariners? Submarines are not sexy like fighter planes; they do not perform at air shows like the Snowbirds; they do not have many books written about them, and Canadian submarines do not have movies made about them. The navy has never promoted submarines in the way that the air force has promoted the Snowbirds, partly because it is difficult to do so and partly because the service operates much of the time clandestinely. And indeed many naval personnel know little about the long and colourful history of their own Submarine Service.

Canada's entry into the submarine business was unplanned, almost accidental. The day WWI broke out, the government of British Columbia bought two primitive boats precipitately to defend the west coast of Canada against two German cruisers that were menacing the north Pacific. This astonishing action on the part of a provincial premier was taken without federal authority and caused a great stir in Ottawa and Victoria. The boats were smuggled out of their Seattle shipyard at dead of night and were nearly shelled by trigger-happy militia on arrival in Esquimalt. That arrival day, August 5th, is the Canadian Submarine Service's birthday, though it is rarely remembered and never celebrated.

From that day forward the Canadian submariners have recognized the tactical value of submarines and have endeavoured to maintain their inclusion in the Canadian fleet. Their efforts have been determined and persistent but not always effective; because up until 1945, sometimes the naval brass and frequently the federal government held the belief that the British Empire would provide submarines for us. Post-WWII the politicians have been teasingly slow to understand and support a Canadian Submarine Service, but non-submariners in the navy came to embrace submarines fully by the 1980s.

The Royal Canadian Navy manned the first submarines in the summer of 1914 with mostly amateur sailors and endeavoured to use the boats as deterrents around the southwest coast of Canada. Records show that *CC1* and *CC2* did not frighten the Germans away--they were not heading for British Columbia--but the submarines certainly calmed the fears of the inhabitants of Victoria and Vancouver when they felt most vulnerable. Within a few months the German threat evaporated and the boats led a much quieter existence while some of their officers transferred overseas, eager to see more action.

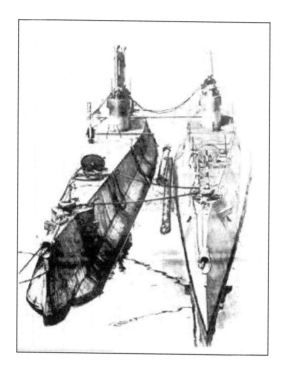

Canada's first submarines, CC1 and CC2, in 1914.

(Credit: DND/PA-1133254)

After *CC1* and *CC2* began patrolling the west coast in WWI, Vickers of Montreal built twenty-four H class boats for Britain, Italy, and Russia in record time giving Canada an early headstart in submarine construction, which few shipyards in the world could claim at that time. Sadly the nation did not capitalize on the capability after WWI.

In 1917, the British Admiralty, needing more submarines for the Mediterranean theatre, asked for *CC1* and *CC2*. The submarines set off on an epic voyage from Victoria to Halifax and gained some fame for being the first naval vessels to sail through the newly opened Panama Canal, and some notoriety for their continual breakdowns. When they limped into Halifax their diesel engines were wrecked and they never went any further east. After surviving the deadly Halifax Explosion and having a major refit, *CC1* and *CC2* took part in the earliest passive sonar testing and training the RCN ever did. Alexander Graham Bell observed the whole procedure and may have been involved in an official capacity but the original records have been destroyed so we can never be sure.

With the war's end, the first Canadian submarines were mothballed and never sailed again. A second pair of boats, *CH14* and *CH15*, entered the RCN briefly after WWI when Britain handed them over to Canada as a thank-you present. They sailed for a summer and then suffered the same fate as *CC1* and *CC2* after the navy was effectively emasculated by under-funding between the wars. *CH14* and *CH15*'s demise signaled the disappearance of submarines from the fleet for forty years, *but not the requirement.*

Reaction to the horror of the First World War was part of the reason that Canada did not nurture her navy during the inter-war period. WWI was, after all, the war to end all wars and had thoroughly scared everyone--and scared everyone into forgetting the importance of preparedness. Nations did away with the weapons of war as fast as they could and most of the combatant nations were short of funds. Another reason our navy declined was that although Canada was thirsting for independence from the British Empire we still looked to Britain for security. Politicians believed that the mother country would continue to protect us, although Britain was decreasing her presence around the world. Also, we must remember that at that time nations and navies still undervalued submarines--they were considered "ungentlemanly"-- and, worse yet, they threatened to take some of the prestige and money away from the mighty surface fleets. WW1's peace dividend was disarmament and nowhere was it more evident than Canada. Our navy shrank to three ships and 500 officers and men in 1920, despite the navy's stated requirement for thirty-three destroyers and four submarines. Anti-submarine warfare (ASW), though appreciated, was not a Canadian priority at all.

Lack of vision and isolationism caught Canada with her pants down yet again in 1939 when the Second World War was declared. The fleet barely met peacetime requirements--there were two destroyers and two minesweepers in Halifax and four destroyers and two minesweepers in Esquimalt. Canada still had no submarines, no submarine experience, and no submariners despite the stated requirement. Worse yet, what fleet there was had never trained with a live submarine and had only four asdic sets (the forerunner of modern passive sonar) between the ships. Everyone knows that the RCN fought the Battle of the Atlantic, that it grew to be the world's third largest navy, and that it was made up of nothing but surface ships. Few know that from 1940 on the RCN had to use borrowed submarines in Canadian waters to train the escort groups to do battle with the U-boats. Canada's lack of submarines was never resolved even at the end of the war.

The naval archives are full of memos and letters from operational commanders screaming for submarines to provide target services to their escort groups for ASW training, as well as dozens of pleas from naval headquarters to the British Admiralty for submarines to borrow. The desperation derived from the RCN's failure to foresee the requirement to protect the Allied convoys from U-boats in the Atlantic. They also believed that Britain would assume this responsibility if indeed unrestricted submarine warfare actually materialized. In fact, the RCN was so desperate for ASW training in 1940 that when a Dutch submarine, which had avoided capture when Holland was invaded, fetched up in Halifax *en route* to England, the navy used it without permission and would not let it go when the Admiralty asked them to relinquish her. Soon 700 officers and 1500 men each year needed ASW training and Britain, so severely stretched by the conflict, simply did not have the hulls to provide to us. Our top brass talked over the possibility of establishing a Canadian Submarine Service, once in 1942 and twice in 1943, but never could break away from their surface mentality--they kept ordering more corvettes. Thus a golden opportunity slid away, the cupboard remained bare, and the escort group commanders continued fighting not only the U-boats but also naval headquarters.

By the end of the war, fourteen aging British submarines had served the Canadian cause, but never all at once. Many had a new generation of Canadian submariners serving in them, one boat had been handed over to the Royal Canadian Air Force to train their aircrews, and all had contributed to the navy's understanding of underwater sound propagation, which was in its infancy and incredibly difficult, especially in our shallow waters. However, their greatest contribution had been to prove, without a doubt, that a fleet is only half a fleet without submarines.

Fatigue, variety, and hard conditions were the lot of the Canadians who chose to serve in submarines in the Second World War, spiced with occasional excitement and infrequent terror. All were volunteer reservists and some, foreseeing war, had enrolled early. The rest were propelled into signing up after the Nazis swept through Western Europe in 1940. The twenty-six Canadians who opted to serve in submarines were ordinary young men and had no idea what they were letting themselves in for. They came from "sea to shining sea" and from every walk of life. None of the twenty-six individuals, all officers, considered going into submarines--boats were their second or even third choices after aircraft carriers and motor torpedo boats. They served in full size submarines, in midget submarines called X-craft, and in "human torpedoes" or chariots. They served in every theatre of WWII, from Canadian waters to the South China Sea; from the Mediterranean to the Arctic approaches. Several commanded submarines and a handful were decorated. The majority loved their time in submarines. However only one opted to stay in submarines after the war and he went on to become the first commander of the reborn Canadian Submarine Service in the 1960s.

Penury and the rapid deflation of the RCN after the war were the major reasons Canada did not act on the hard-learned ASW lessons of WWII and did not acquire submarines. The navy certainly tried but the politicians, who wanted nothing more of capital ships, fighting, or expense, blew their post-war plans for a blue water fleet out of the water. It is hard to believe but submarines did not become a part of our fleet again until 1961.

Canada joined the United Nations with hope for a better world and NATO for joint protection if it turned sour again. We chose to make ASW the navy's specialty to gain a little more influence at the new joint tables of power, but still did not buy submarines, even though the training requirements for the fleet and the RCAF had reached enormous proportions. When in the 1950s the RCN needed 1000 submarine training days each year, the minister of national defence was heard to say that Canada had no intention of establishing a submarine arm of the Royal Canadian Navy.

A glimmer of understanding broke through the gloom when the government agreed to rent a whole submarine squadron from the Royal Navy, but the decision perpetuated our reliance on an outside agency instead of developing the necessary expertise and independence at home. The first boat of the Sixth Submarine Squadron (SM6) arrived in Halifax in April 1955, ten years after the war had ended, and the squadron stayed until 1966. Although shown by archival documents to be unintentional, the agreement with Britain for SM6 provided the RCN with a core of qualified submariners that enabled the RCN to man the small new submarine branch of the '60s. The original contract called for 200 officers and men to be sent to the RN to be trained for service in British submarines in return for the squadron.

Just before SM6 arrived in Halifax, the Americans launched their first nuclear-powered submarine (SSN), USS *Nautilus,* and changed the underwater world forever, putting a whole new spin on submarine procurement, cost, and operations. The RCN's studies resulting from this momentous event delayed the acquisition of our own submarines, but in the late 1950s the navy did finally succeed in proving the value of submarines to the politicians. They did this by eclipsing their value as ASW platforms and by emphasizing the training assistance they could give to the surface fleet. However, it was not until 1961 that one "new-to-you" diesel/electric submarine, HMCS *Grilse,* came alongside in Esquimalt and spearheaded the restoration of the modern Canadian submarine era. Since then the Canadian navy has had between one and three boats continuously in the fleet.

Cold War tensions, the ASW training needs of the Canadian fleet and aircrews, and Britain's announcement to gradually withdraw SM6 had forced the politicians into approving submarines for our navy. The prospect of improving Canada's contribution to NATO and, with it, gaining more influence at the table had not escaped them either. The availability of our RN-trained submariners made it easier and cheaper to start up again and the RCN used them to tip the balance. The navy obtained *Grilse* for the cost of reactivation only, on the understanding that she would return to the United States Navy. She was a WWII fleet boat, palatial in comparison to anything the Canadian submariners had experienced in the British navy, and had been built for the war in the Pacific. HMCS *Rainbow* followed *Grilse* in 1968, also from the USN, but was an outright purchase. Based in Esquimalt too, she provided tame submarine services to the west coast fleet and participated in multi-national exercises in the Pacific, but did no operational patrols. Surveillance was not viewed as a primary Canadian submarine role at the time.

Emphasis on the training of the surface fleet and aircrews remained paramount as the RCN plugged away at getting more boats. Perhaps it was a more acceptable reason for the politicians to embrace, but it led to a Canadian Submarine Service that was viewed as a training aid for years and years. After their unsuccessful flirtation with nuclear-powered submarines in the early '60s, the RCN recommended that Canada acquire twelve diesel/electric boats. Getting little encouragement from the government, the navy weakened their proposal on successive submissions and ended up with three submarines and an option in the future for three more. Of course, the second batch of three was a government sop, an illusion. Diefenbaker's Tory Cabinet approved the purchase of British Oberon class boats, not a popular choice with the submariners, and then postponed it. Soon afterwards, Lester Pearson's Liberals won a general election, Paul Hellyer became the defence minister, and the navy realized the submarine acquisition was in serious jeopardy.

Hellyer's defence review scared everyone, but in late 1963 the three proposed submarines were reinstated. The official announcements stressed that the boats were to be used for training purposes only but were also fully operational as ASW weapons platforms. By mid-1964 a Canadian team was in Britain overseeing the construction of HMCS *Ojibwa, Onondaga*, and *Okanagan.* The submarines all arrived in Canada by 1968 and now the navy had a submarine fleet of two nationalities--American on the west coast and British on the east, a situation that created all kinds of logistic, personnel, and training challenges.

The arrival of HMCS Grilse heralded the rebirth of a submarine branch in the Canadian navy in 1961.
(Credit: Department of National Defence)

When the First Canadian Submarine Squadron was officially formed in 1966, its primary job was to provide target services to the fleet, a role that has taken years to enlarge. From day one, Canadian submariners have endeavoured to educate the fleet as to the value of their boats but have had to earn their spurs repeatedly. When their tenacity and dedication finally began to pay off in the '80s and the navy was thinking in terms of multi-platform operations, the O boats were past their prime. Today the submarines and their crews rate their operational patrols conducting surveillance in the Canadian zone of the Atlantic and covert missions (for the Department of Fisheries and Oceans, for example) as their primary roles. Recently our First Canadian Submarine Squadron was absorbed into the Fifth Maritime Operations Group (MOG5), which is led by a submariner. They now participate in multi-national exercises, not only as training targets, but also as fully-fledged team members. If world tensions rise, Canadian boats will intensify their surveillance of shipping, and in any NATO conflicts would join their submarine pool for use as hunter/killers in classified locations, but only if the Canadian government allows them to do so. Of course with just three submarines acquired from 1966 to 1998, their important surveillance work could only be achieved intermittently in the Atlantic and not at all in the Pacific. Amazingly enough, despite the growing importance of the Asia-Pacific region, no submarine has served on the Canadian west coast since the mid-1970s.

Although never enough for the huge maritime responsibilities Canada has to manage, these few submarines have been sufficient to maintain the essential expertise and to build a strong service with a worldwide reputation, which is accepted as an equal by the

**The three Oberon class submarines alongside in Halifax after their up-date, 1986.
L to R: HMCS Okanagan, Onondaga, and Ojibwa.**

(Credit: Department of National Defence)

international submarine community. The First Canadian Submarine Squadron has been instrumental in the maturation of the top-notch surveillance skills of our anti-submarine warfare navy since the mid-60s, as well as the provision of the essential balance our financially constrained navy must have.

For the past fifteen years, the navy has been attempting to get new boats to replace the aging Oberons. It has been a frustrating task--on-again, off-again, sometimes diesel/electric and sometimes nuclear-powered. In 1985, the navy finally got the go-ahead to identify the conventional submarine they wanted and to build them onshore. A new Conservative government changed the playing field, cancelled the diesel/electric program, and brought in the nuclear-powered submarine program--ten to twelve SSNs for $5 billion. After that fell apart, and with it the 1987 Defence White Paper, the Department of National Defence again looked at replacing the old boats, but this time with four second-hand British diesel/electric boats which could be had at little or no cost. Canada did not act with all speed and the Brits, wondering if we would let them down again, resorted to showing several other nations their wares. If we had missed this opportunity, there were no other cheap, suitable submarines available in the world and Canada would have lost her submarine branch of the navy.

Canada now has nearly forty years of modern submarine experience and the navy has gained much from it. The Cold War honed the Canadian submariners' skills and, by the end of it, they had earned a well-deserved reputation for ASW at home and abroad. Overseas, NATO eagerly seeks them out to participate in major maritime exercises and to be part of allied submarine contingency plans. Navies with only nuclear-powered submarines, which find the skills difficult to practise, envy our growing expertise in difficult shallow water operations. Our submariners have also nurtured a cooperative relationship with the aircrews of the shipborne helicopters and fixed-wing maritime patrol aircraft, which provide the "long legs" component of effective surveillance and ASW in the Canadian zone of the North Atlantic. This has developed into a significant bond, which, by contrast, they do not feel as much with the surface crews. It is well known that if you can master and excel in ASW, you can do everything else well too. At home, Canadian submariners have also enhanced the country's scientific, research and development, exploration, and industrial communities in undersea endeavours by providing expertise, personnel, and platforms. This enormous reputation for such a small component of the navy is astounding when one realizes what little support the submarine branch has received throughout their chequered history. Not only are their skills a valuable asset to the navy, they even give Canada some increased influence at the UN and in NATO, quite out of proportion to our overall contributions, which are viewed as less than they should be.

Our submarine heritage has also had a hand in making Canada a world-leader in commercial sub-sea technology. Some of the best remotely operated underwater vehicles, similar to the ones used to discover and explore the wreck of RMS *Titanic*, are designed and built by International Submarine Engineering Ltd. in British Columbia. Canadian sonars for small submersibles compete with the best in the world. Phil Nuyten of Hard Suits Inc. in North Vancouver designed the diving suit that looks a bit like a Michelin Man known as the NuytSuit. Not far away in Burnaby, Ballard Power Systems is developing an air-independent propulsion system for diesel/electric submarines so that they can operate under the Arctic ice. Their fuel cell research, seeded by funds from the Department of National Defence (DND), is causing a stir in the world automotive industry as well and Ballard has signed contracts with Daimler-Benz and other car manufacturers to develop it for use in cars and buses.

It is an inescapable fact that our submarines have provided a remarkable return on investment over the years, being the least costly of all major naval platforms to buy and operate. At one-third the operating cost of a modern frigate and with the lowest vulnerability quotient, our few aging submarines have exerted a formidable presence. This presence exists whether they are there or not--they just have to be perceived as "possibly being there." As a consequence, foreign fishing vessels are never quite sure if they may encounter a Canadian submarine on the Grand Banks and drug runners know they could be filmed through the periscope, at least on the Atlantic side of Canada. The Oberons of the First Canadian Submarine Squadron cost $30 million a year (1997 figures) to operate, which represented less than 0.03% of the federal budget and only about 2% of naval operations and maintenance money.

Few Canadians are aware we have submarines and fewer still know what they have given to the navy and to our nation. Almost no one seems to care either--except the submariners and surface sailors of our present navy. Submarines apparently still carry the stigma of the U-boats--nasty, silent, killers of innocent merchant sailors and passengers--and Canadians want no part of that. Neither the Canadian Submarine Service nor the navy has done much to combat this public attitude and the promotion they have done for our submarines and submariners does not seem to have had much effect on the average Canadian. Granted, its difficult to do with submarines what the air force has achieved with the Snowbirds.

On the other hand, the promotional efforts have had significant impact internally from the 1980s on. The three naval components--on, over, and under the sea--became much more mutually supporting in operations and, fortunately, in acquisition matters. Indeed, much of the credit for the acquisition of the new Victoria class boats can be given to non-submariners, both the surface sailors and the maritime air community, for their whole-hearted belief and success in multi-platform surveillance.

Compounding the negative influences on the submarines' image in Canada is a House of Commons with no defence constituency. Almost no current members of Parliament have ever been in the Canadian Forces and those who are interested in preserving Canada's defence are few.

Talented, independent, stable, self-reliant, adaptable, and compatible are some of the traits that characterized the successful Canadian submariner of 1914 and 1940, and they are just as necessary today. Our modern submariners must have the intelligence and skills to master the highly sophisticated technologies found in modern submarine systems as well. To our credit, Canada continuously produces outstanding submariners who are determined and willing to make-do and who perform well in the singularly adverse conditions of our northern oceans. They are risk-takers all--indeed in the words of one non-Canadian submarine commentator, "Canadian submariners are first-rate, aggressive and innovative.[1]" Just as there is a similarity between fighter aircraft and submarines, and Top Gun and Perisher,* so there is between pilots and submariners. From the first rookie crews of CC1 and CC2, to the highly-educated, trained teams of today, each man has played a part in making a very small component successful in a navy that has, in the past, seen itself floating predominately on the surface.

For the first twenty-five years of the modern era, Canadians who served in boats did so entirely voluntarily--submariners around the world prided themselves on the volunteer nature of their calling as it was thought to attract only those of the highest calibre. However, statistics show that submarines were not often the first choice of individuals. Many of the men chose submarines for a change: "...the training and experience were good, the travel varied, and the responsibilities and challenges greater."[2]

Many officers had had their initial aspirations in the navy foiled and were attracted by the prospect of early command in submarines. But only a very few regretted their choice. Sadly, a career in Canadian submarines has not been so enticing recently due to their uncertain future, so, to keep the submarines fully manned, the navy decided to modify the volunteer nature of the branch in 1986. The new policy allowed both officers and men to be conscripted into the submarines to top up the ships' complements. Contrary to gloomy forecasts that conscripts would dilute the elite spirit of the Canadian Submarine Service, the policy turned out to have the opposite effect--many pressed into service caught the bug and later volunteered to remain in submarines. The majority of Canadian submariners, volunteers and conscripts alike, are fiercely proud of their service, gleefully delighted to be a part of it, and intensely motivated to do a first-rate, professional job.

As a maritime nation, Canada cannot afford to throw away this hard-won expertise and spirit, this investment, and this asset that has developed and strengthened over the last eighty-six years. Instead, we should be celebrating our proud submarine heritage and tradition loudly enough for all to hear.

*Top Gun is the US course for its top fighter pilots that Canadians also attend and have occasionally finished in first place. The Canadian and British Perisher teaches prospective submarine captains the art and science of underwater attack. The courses are considered to be the toughest in the world, as well as the most expensive. Both push their participants to the outer limits of their endurance and skill

Chapter Two
CANADA'S DEFENCE POLICY

*"...a nation not worth defending is
a nation not worth preserving."*

Before we tackle the issue of retaining submarines in the Canadian navy, we need to step back and examine Canada's defence policy--what it is and why we have one. The Canadian Forces cannot itself provide the justification for submarines, but the government's defence policy can. If we can establish the need for our armed forces and especially the navy, we can then proceed to explain why Canada needs submarines in the new millennium.

Defence policy flows primarily from our sovereignty--our independent nationhood--as well as from our desire for world peace within the context of international alliances. The Department of Foreign Affairs and International Trade (DFAIT) determines the government's policies regarding Canada's sovereignty and international relations. Canada has another, less philanthropic but vitally important, interest in preserving world peace--our economic future depends upon our ability to trade freely with other nations. World trade has grown enormously and has become intricately interdependent. The European Union and NAFTA are two examples of expanding free trade areas and we will be seeing more. DFAIT, and therefore Canada, believes that international trade advances Canadians' employment and prosperity at home and enhances world stability.

The Department of Foreign Affairs has the lead role for coordinating federal policy related to our sovereignty, including sovereignty over and under Canadian waters. Canada follows the UN Convention on the Law of the Sea (UNCLOS), and has set out the extent of our sovereignty over the oceans in the recently proclaimed Canada's Oceans Act. And, of course, whatever Canada deems sovereign, the Department of National Defence has to protect--and it is a huge area of land and sea, covering over 18 million square kilometers.

However, the cornerstone of our foreign policy is the protection of our nation's security within a stable global framework. Canadian security at home depends more than ever on that of others--our interdependence with the rest of the world is growing with the acceleration in globalization, technological development, and the scale of human activity. However, it would be wrong to imply that Canadians are only into peace just for ourselves--our desire to build peace for others reflects some of the most deeply held and widely shared Canadian values, and ones we would fight for at that.

While the Department of Foreign Affairs naturally stresses the use of diplomacy to deal with threats of all sorts, from military ones to over-population, it also firmly states that Canada's overall security policy must include provision for adequate defence of our nation and citizens, as well as those abroad who are victims of oppression. Our memberships in the joint security organizations of NATO and NORAD remain our key guarantees of military security for our country, though at the moment a direct threat to North America is unlikely. NORAD has enabled Canada to share the burden of North American defence for many years at significantly less cost and with greater effectiveness than if we had done it alone and it has provided a steady forum for Canadian influence in continental deliberations.

The UN, on the other hand, is Canada's main vehicle for pursuing global objectives of stability and security. The success of the UN is fundamental to the world and Canada's future security and we are doing as much as we can to strengthen the UN's rapid reaction policy and administration, as well as to enhance other measures to stabilize the world. For example, Canada is one nation among several that has established a centre for the training of international personnel for peacekeeping operations.

However, Canada does not rely solely on the United Nations for her efforts to promote world peace, for we are actively involved in other ways too. Regionally, Canada is fully engaged--the Arctic and the Asia-Pacific region have demanded our attention and received it in increasing amounts. The government has appointed an Ambassador for Circumpolar Affairs and is hoping to establish an Arctic Council to meet the increasingly non-traditional security issues in the north and to deal with critical matters faced by all Arctic countries, not the least of which is pollution. The Asia-Pacific region also poses serious security challenges close enough to home to be worrying--human rights abuses, weapons proliferation, population growth, illegal immigration, and narcotics trafficking are issues that come to mind--and Canada is actively working with other nations to ensure peace and security prevail around the Pacific.

Canada, through DFAIT, has been and is in the forefront of world initiatives to combat the growth of all types of weapons--our leadership on the landmine issue is a prime example. However, although much has already been done to reduce the world's nuclear arsenals, DFAIT is aware that nations in South Asia and the Middle East are working on their nuclear capabilities. The threat of terrorists possessing these and other weapons of destruction is of growing concern to all Canadians.[3]

So it is easy to see, with the Department of Foreign Affairs defining Canada's sovereign territory and developing policies which define our relationship with the world, why defence policy must come after foreign policy. Our Department of National Defence is the instrument with which we protect and promote ourselves and our partners, thus upholding the doctrine of our foreign policy.

The need for fiscal restraint and departmental cutbacks strongly influenced the development and content of Canada's latest defence policy, announced by the Liberals in early 1994, along with a strong advocacy for continued involvement within our means in peacekeeping operations around the world. The 1994 White Paper on Defence[4] was the result of a lengthy and in-depth review process and the inter-related work of the Special Joint Committee of the Senate and House of Commons on Canada's Defence Policy. This multi-party committee sat for many months hearing submissions from Canadians of all stripes on all aspects of defence. In the introduction to the 1994, White Paper on Defence the defence minister wrote that nearly all the committee's recommendations were met.[5] However, the government did not accept the committee's suggestion regarding the size of the Canadian Forces, as they believed their ideas were inconsistent with the funds available.

While foreign policy can, and sometimes does, change very quickly in response to world events, defence policy and its programs cannot. With some equipment lead times as long as fifteen years, it is a slow-moving creature at best. Defence policy has to be based, not on desires for peace, but on events and trends in the outside world and what they mean or may mean to Canada. It is always a "best guess" proposition and, when coupled with lack of funds, planning policy and programs is a very difficult process indeed.

As most recent defence policies have done, the 1994 policy explains that the fundamental mission of the Department of National Defence is **to defend Canada and Canadian interests** and values while contributing to international peace and security. The primacy of national sovereignty makes the policy more "inward-looking than Canadian foreign policy"[6] and slightly different from the defence policies of the Cold War era, when collective security was the priority.

Defending our sovereignty means that we must ensure that Canadian law is respected and enforced by monitoring and controlling activity within our jurisdiction. This jurisdiction includes, not only our landmass, but also our airspace, our coastlines, our oceans, and our citizens wherever they may be. If we allow this responsibility to fall to others by choice or by default, we are no longer a sovereign state. In several polls, Canadians have made it abundantly clear that we are committed to the protection of our country, our people, and our resources.[7] The strong reaction of the media and our citizens to the voyage of the *Polar Sea* through the North West Passage and the depletion of turbot stocks by the Spanish are prime examples of our true feelings when it comes to sovereignty violations. However this begs the question: do Canadians think that being angry is enough or are we prepared to pay for trained personnel and equipment to fight for what is ours?

The reduction in the threat of global war has not reduced the role of the Canadian Forces at home; indeed, it has grown. Well into the next century, the Canadian government requires the armed forces to provide, along with other government agencies, many vital services. One of these is effective Aid of the Civil Power-- although rarely used, provinces have the right to call upon the Canadian Forces to assist in maintaining or restoring order when it is beyond their ability to do so. The Oka crisis is a good example of this function. Canada must also maintain the ability to evacuate Canadian nationals from areas threatened by imminent conflict. The CF is responsible for the nation's air search and rescue capability and operates three Rescue Coordination Centres across the country. The Department of National Defence reluctantly absorbed the agency for emergency preparedness and, in so doing, has become responsible for disaster relief and must be able to provide humanitarian assistance within 24 hours anywhere in the country. The floods in Manitoba in 1997 and the devastating ice storm in Quebec and eastern Ontario in January 1998 used thousands of troops to provide urgent help to millions of Canadians in need. The CF also plays a significant role in countering illegal drug running and immigration--one of our submarines was instrumental in gathering the evidence that resulted in the biggest heroin seizure in Canadian history and the successful prosecution of the traffickers. Hand in hand with the Department of the Environment, National Defence is now also involved in environmental surveillance, pollution control, especially in our oceans, and clean up.

The involvement of the CF in seemingly non-military roles may seem a poor use of military hardware and personnel but is, in fact, a good use of resources in a fiscally constrained era. To have separate fleets for the Departments of Transport, the RCMP, and the Coastguard (when you can share vessels) is no longer affordable. This compromise may not be ideal in every instance, but it is the new reality.

Second only to the protection of Canada, our defence policy addresses **the defence of North America** in partnership with the United States. This is a highly valued and important facet of our defence posture--together we form a major area of stability in a turbulent world and it has been proven over the last fifty years to work well. The North American Aerospace Defence Agreement (NORAD) is the best-known feature of the cooperative effort. With a fully integrated US/Canadian headquarters, NORAD controls the air defence of North America. Less well known are the many other bilateral agreements that cover everything from the promotion of Arctic security and joint operations and communications, to intelligence sharing, training and logistics, and even defence production. Canada gains hugely from these agreements while retaining a voice in the joint defence planning and practice. The maritime dimension of the Canada-US Basic Security Plan[8] involves the surveillance and control of vast areas in the Atlantic and Pacific, as well as in the Arctic Ocean. To achieve this, two joint (Canada/US) maritime task groups have been created on both coasts of the North American continent.

Thirdly, Canada promises to continue to be a strong **advocate of multilateral institutions.** We belong to the United Nations, NATO, the Group of Seven (eight if we include Russia), the GATT, the Commonwealth, la Francophonie, the Organization of American States, the Asia-Pacific Economic Cooperation forum, and the Conference on Security and Cooperation in Europe (CSCE)*This involvement is ongoing, whether or not we have

---

*CSCE is the only organization addressing regional security concerns in Europe that includes Russia and nearly all the countries of Central and Eastern Europe, even though at present it lacks an effective decision-making mechanism.

personnel serving abroad on peacekeeping missions, because of our belief that collaboration eases the burden both financially and morally. To this end Canada supplies one ship to the Standing Naval Force Atlantic at all times and occasionally contributes one ship to the Standing Naval Force Mediterranean, personnel for the NATO Airborne Early Warning system, 200 personnel for various NATO headquarters, and provides opportunities for allied forces to conduct training in Canada on a cost-recovery basis.

"Canada... has been an active player in the recent surge of UN operations"[9] and government support of these and NATO **peacekeeping** missions will continue to assist in the promotion of stability and security in the world, as it has historically. These types of operations are some of the best-known and best-supported functions of the Department of National Defence these days and generate the most pride in the Canadian Forces from a population usually disinterested in "things military." Peacekeeping ranges from the traditional observer roles, to the prevention of escalation of minor conflicts, post-conflict peacebuilding and restoration of devastated areas, the enforcement of sanctions or arms embargoes, the restoration of order to ensure the delivery of humanitarian aid, enforcement of "no-fly zones", the protection of "safe" areas, and to the deterrence or defence of a member state against armed attack. From the point of view of hardware and personnel, our current defence policy requires Canada to contribute a naval task force that could include submarines, fighter and transport planes, and large numbers of ground forces to multilateral operations. In practice, Canada has to be selective over which operations we can join due to our limited resources, often inadequate equipment, and other peacekeeping commitments around the globe. The Department of National Defence also continues to support and contribute to the enhancement of training of peacekeeping personnel internationally by operating the Lester B. Pearson Canadian International Peacekeeping Training Centre in the Maritimes.

Neglected over the years, the **Asia-Pacific region** is growing so fast it is changing the balance of the world significantly. Asia is now so much a part of Canadian culture, especially in the west, that we need to be intimately involved with it in the new century. A few facts emphasize the implications to Canadians: by 2000 the region will have 60% of the world's population, 50% of the world's production, and 40% of the world's total consumption. In 1993 Canada exported $16.6 billion worth of goods to Asia-Pacific (BC alone contributing $6.8 billion annually) and imported $25.1 billion worth, making us second only to the United States in oriental trade. Furthermore, our ties to the region are strengthening as a result of the immigration from Korea, Taiwan, Hong Kong, and Singapore.

With the growing importance of the Pacific Rim, Canada's latest defence policy recognizes the need for collective defence arrangements like NATO in the Asia-Pacific region, as well as the importance of stability in the area. To this end, DFAIT participates in the Asia Regional Forum, APEC, and the Association of South East Asian Nations (ASEAN), etc. Further, the Special Joint Committee on Defence recommended: "...if we are to have influence in the region, in security terms as well as economic ones, we must see and be seen, we must demonstrate a more visible Canadian presence in the Pacific waters...." The Department of National Defence has already deployed ships to the region and plans to continue to do so--to Northeast Asia in even years and Southeast Asia in odd years. In addition, there will be Canadian naval exercises with the Chilean and Peruvian navies. The Asian navies seem reluctant to follow suit. Japan does however participate in the naval and air exercise called RIMPAC, along with the USA, Canada and Australia, but this does not provide multilateral training opportunities so necessary for UN-style operations.

The government, through DND, also plans to increase Canada's participation in regional security dialogues in the Asia-Pacific area, but there is little in place yet to provide the structure and the comfort zone Canada is used to in the Atlantic region. We need to be aware that there are factors present in the Pacific basin that have traditionally led to conflict and war--we see "resource-rich states and those that are poor and ambitious,"[10] democracies and dictatorships, exploding populations, and rapidly growing armed forces. With closer Canadian ties to Asia-Pacific, responsibilities similar to those that come with our membership in NATO and the UN will undoubtedly emerge to claim our attention and perhaps our intervention. This is the cost of international cooperation and security maintenance.

In the fiscal year 1998-99 the federal government allotted $9.38 billion to the Department of National Defence to implement this policy, including the defence department roles at home. This was a drop of 27% from the $12.03 billion of five years before and was 6% lower than previously planned, although deployment of CF personnel was at its highest since the Korean War. Most of the reduction has come from cuts in the capital program and personnel reductions (from 86,000 in 1989 to 60,000 in 2000)[11]. In contrast the world's military spending has dropped only 14% below its level of *seventeen* years ago. However, for the first time since the early 90s, Canada's defence budget started to increase slightly in FY 1998-99. (For a comparison of defence spending with other government's expenditures, see Table 1.)

Project Ploughshares, a group actively opposed to further defence spending, believes that DND could perform its duties for only $7.5-8.0 billion annually as long as equipment like helicopters and submarines are not replaced.[12] However, it is a known fact that money saved on defence in peacetime is directly related to lives lost in subsequent conflicts, often because of out-dated and inadequate equipment and training. This sobering thought should make every MP very cautious when voting for defence cuts and should make every Canadian think twice when supporting them, in light of the government's inclination for sending our troops on almost every peacekeeping operation out there. Recent reductions in defence spending meant that our peacekeepers were sent to the highly dangerous theatre in Bosnia with thirty-year-old armoured personnel carriers that were long overdue for replacement

In 1991 Canada spent 1.4% of our GDP on defence--ranking our defence spending 93rd in the world--a percentage of GDP that had not changed by the end of the millennium. The Maritime Command portion of our annual defence budget was $1.8 billion or 18.5% in FY1999-00.To put the total naval investment into better perspective, it represents 1.8% of the $115.5 billion federal budget (1999-00). In contrast, Canada spends five times more on debt reduction charges than on defence, 90% more on transfer payments and subsidies, and spent $35 billion in 1999-00 on employment insurance and old age pensions. If we think our citizens deserve to

Year	Total federal budget	EI and OAP	Defence budget	Annual deficit	Net debt
1994-95	118.7	35.3	11.8	37.5	545.7
1995-96	112.0	34.5	11.08	28.6	574.3
1996-97	109.0	34.7	10.5	19.0	593.3
1997-98	108.8	35.8	9.25	14.0	579.7
1998-99	111.4	37.0	9.38	(11.5)	576.8
1999-00	115.5	35.0	10.3	(8.0)	?
2000-01	116	36.0	10.43	5.0	?

Table 1: Comparison of government expenditures and debt in billions of dollars
(Figures in parentheses denote a surplus)

be financially supported when jobless or aging, why don't we perceive that we deserve to be protected adequately, especially when the cost is so reasonable in comparison?

For this investment of nearly $2 billion, Canada's navy attempts to meet all the responsibilities the government puts upon it. We operate sixteen destroyers and frigates, three replenishment ships, a few mine-countermeasure ships, several smaller vessels for coastal patrol, diving and training, and, up to September 1998, our three Oberon submarines. Air Command's maritime air group operates both shipborne helicopters and shore-based fixed-wing patrol *Aurora* (18) and *Arcturus* (3) aircraft. All assets, except the submarines, are deployed on both coasts, but there is nothing in the Arctic. Canada's navy currently has about 9000 regular force personnel and 4000 reservists, down from a 15,000 total in 1994.

This is a summary of Canada's current defence policy and what it costs, but it gives little idea as to the true size and scope of our security responsibilities at home and abroad, or about how the Department of National Defence implements the policy with personnel and equipment. Only by looking at the uniqueness of Canada and the present and future state of the world, can we really see what is needed in the way of a navy and submarines.

Over the last couple of decades, it has become fashionable to criticize the Department of National Defence, the CF, and our military equipment, rather than celebrate what they have done for the world and for this country. Some of the more loudly expressed arguments against Canadian defence include: Canada should be neutral; we would make better use of limited funds by spending them on social programs or on the third world; and there is no threat to Canada any more.

Several well-known Canadians and the federal National Democratic Party have flirted with the option of making Canada neutral. However, public opinion does not support the idea. Canadians have made it quite clear that they desire a means to protect the country, and its interests abroad, with armed forces. We wish also to continue our involvement in peacekeeping and alliances. If Canada adopts a neutral or isolationist stance, we will lose our ties and our credibility with our allies and will have to "go it alone." This way of protecting ourselves would be much more costly than by "sharing" the burden with NATO and the USA. If the neutralist lobby means to do away with our Department of National Defence altogether, we would then forfeit our sovereignty, our willingness to promote peace with freedom for ourselves and for others around the world, and we might be absorbed into another country.

Peace lobbies and the more left wing political parties also argue that the Canadian government "...would make better use of limited funds by concentrating on human and environmental needs."[13] Social programs are vital to our nation but do not remove the need to sustain a Canadian presence on the fishing grounds, to provide domestic disaster relief, or to monitor our sovereignty. Nor do social services remove Canadian citizens' expressed desire for Canada to be an active peacekeeper. The government has already cut nearly $10 billion from the defence budgets since the 1980s, but expects the Department of National Defence to meet more responsibilities with an increased peacekeeping component. And never, at any time, has any government diverted money from social programs or foreign aid to defence.

The argument for tackling the world tensions through improving the lot of people in the third world is one that Canada is viewing with interest, despite a recent reduction in foreign aid. Some politicians would like to divert money, normally used for defence, to development assistance programs overseas in the belief that it is poverty and malnutrition that causes global unrest and instability. This theory may have some merit in certain circumstances but is far from proven and should be treated with caution--generally it is greedy leaders who tip the world's balance off kilter and not the impoverished and sick.

Since the Cold War ended and the clearly defined enemy, the Soviet bloc, has dissolved, there are groups like Canada 21* who feel that Canada's defence policy does not reflect this new reality.[14] They want the government to concentrate on bolstering our peacekeeping abilities by increasing the numbers of Canadian ground troops and modernizing their equipment, and by reducing the navy and airforce to a kind of home defence force to protect our territorial sovereignty. Certainly this will garner brownie points from those nations calling for peacekeeping help and, may be for a while, from our citizens but it has some drawbacks.

To concentrate on peacekeeping in an era of diminishing funds can only mean reducing and/or eliminating some of the military's traditional capabilities, such as ASW, and equipment, like submarines.

This suggestion also leaves the navy out of multinational peacekeeping operations because it will no longer have the vessels with which to participate. Previously our maritime forces have been important parts of the Canadian peacekeeping contributions-- for example, 800 of our sailors were in the Adriatic at the same time as 2000 soldiers were in Bosnia and Canadian ships were responsible for monitoring merchant vessels in the Gulf War. Canada 21's vision also points the way towards Canada becoming the world's peacekeeper and perhaps being left to do it alone while other nations decline to participate. Nor does this type of peacekeeping come cheaply, unless we want to continue the practice of sending our men and women in harm's way with old equipment.

The proposal also seems to forget the immense size of Canadian territory and international trade, as well as the unpredictability of the world in which we live. We simply have to

---

*Canada 21 was a group of politicians, academicians, and media personalities that wrote a critique on the 1994 White Paper on Defence.

prepare for conflict, as much as we would prefer not to, because peacekeeping has evolved into highly dangerous operations with many of the characteristics of all-out war. Well-trained soldiers can step down and do the type of peacekeeping that keeps warring sides apart after a cease-fire is honoured, but well-trained peacekeepers cannot take the step up to fight wars.

Some Canadians suggest that in future we could borrow equipment to replace that which we get rid of should we need it. This is a facile suggestion--our military personnel need it to train on continually at home or they lose their edge. And who is to guarantee the equipment will not be in use when Canada wants it? Furthermore, there is an inherent loss of sovereignty in borrowing that we should avoid.

The Department of National Defence is to Canada what a fire department is to a municipality--insurance and a vehicle for prevention.[15] There are few cities and towns in this country that would disband their fire departments if there had been no fires for a month and, in the same way, we cannot get rid of our defence department because there have been no wars directly involving Canadian territory.

In the end Canada has to develop her defence policy and plan her defence programs by taking into account that which we know to offset that which we do not. We do not know in detail what maritime challenges Canada will face in the 21st century but we *do* know that we are a northern maritime nation surrounded by three oceans, that we are dependent on seaborne trade, that we have many maritime interests, such as fisheries, to protect, and that we belong to collective security organizations like NATO.[16]

While all this explains why we have a Department of National Defence, there are a plethora of other factors involved in explaining why we need a navy with submarines and in planning a defence program. The next step is to consider the state of the planet today and to endeavour to predict, as accurately as we can, the state of the planet five, ten, twenty and thirty years on--the lifespan of a submarine. Then we have to add Canada's geography, our geographical position on the globe, and our limited financial resources to the defence picture. These all complicate the view.

Chapter Three
THE STATE OF THE WORLD

Human nature being what it is has meant that the world has never known an all-encompassing peace, a time with no conflict at all. It seems that man, just like the other animals with which we share our planet, has always fought over partners, possessions, territory, faith, and food. Indeed in centuries gone by, warring was considered a noble calling, as good or better than any other, and in the Middle Ages, it was even thought to earn the warrior a place in heaven if he died fighting the infidel. War was waged regionally in those days and was an intensely personal type of conflict, where soldiers saw the whites of the eyes of their enemies. By the beginning of the 20th century, war was becoming more global in scope and more impersonal. There were times when soldiers faced hand-to-hand combat but most killing was done at a distance. Society at large, too, was involved in wars--world wars put whole countries on a different footing for long periods--and there was a clear differentiation between wartime and peacetime. Nowadays war can be terrifyingly impersonal--with missiles and smart bombs--programmed in a distant land to destroy a specific target at a certain crossroads in an identified city thousands of miles away. The delineation between war and peace has blurred too--during the Gulf War Canada did not consider itself at war, but clearly we were not at peace either.

Warfare, bullying, and downright nastiness seem to be in human genes, and if history is anything to go by, we will continue to see conflicts and fighting, however "civilized" we think we are. Between 1945 and 1989, there have been 138 wars that have killed about 23 million people--a horrifying number--but less than those lost to internal oppression in the same timeframe. Just as there have always been thugs and rogues in every society whose anger, greed, and thirst for power incited their followers to war, there will continue to be such misfits in the new millennium. Regrettably, we have to accept that the world is not always a nice place and that will probably not change, at least in our lifetimes.

War is endemic to the human condition--wars start easily-- and now, without the restraining force of the terrifying consequences of the Cold War, seem likely to be waged with less restraint. The Cold War's culture of controlled tension caused any nation considering the use of force to think twice and is thought to have actually reduced the incidence of "hot" wars. The passing of the Cold War has removed some of the fear that escalation could result in nuclear war and many believe we are entering an era of less restrained and more widespread conventional warfare.

For a moment in the late-80s, humankind was hopeful that a new world order was emerging, driven by people-power, and that the planet would settle into a more peaceful state at last. The collapse of the Berlin Wall, and all that it led to, astonished everyone, sent defence planners into a tailspin, and removed the clearly defined enemy, the Soviets, from the West's traditional bipolar defence equation. However, since 1989 we have seen the emergence of a multi-polar world with much more unexpected nastiness around the globe. Who would have believed that the "ethnic cleansing" in Bosnia and Kosovo, the massive killing in Rwanda's civil war, and Iraq's brutal invasion of Kuwait could happen? Now we face the tension between China and Taiwan, Iraq's ongoing pigheadedness, and the continuing strife in the Middle East. Defence planners ask, "What is the state of the world today? What will come next? And what will the next thirty years bring?"

Most observers of the world scene acknowledge that the 1990's were an inter-war period, meaning that the chances of another world conflagration were slim and that global security was relatively good. All agree that this relative stability could, and most probably will, slide downhill. But even so, the Canadian Forces have been very busy abroad--in fact "five years after the end of the Cold War, Canada [has been] more actively engaged in military terms abroad than at any time in the past forty years."[17] As members of NATO and the UN, we have had troops in most of the multinational forces of the last decade and in the Middle East as active participants in the Gulf War. So in a period of relative peace--and for the first time since the Korean War (and this is vitally important to remember)--we have expected Canadian service men and women to lay their lives on the line. History may not repeat itself in detail but, as Dr. Colin Gray observed, "Bad times will return and there will be 'thugs'... in need of discipline."[18]

What indicators are there which can help us quantify the state of global security at the moment, and what are the chances that a rogue regime will pop up somewhere, sometime? The growing world population is placing increasing pressure on food and energy resources and is damaging the environment at an alarming rate--by the mid-21st century the world will have to support 10 billion people. Growing religious fundamentalism also has to be considered as a factor in the world's security picture. The UN estimates that about 20 million people have been forced to flee their homes as refugees in the last thirteen years. Furthermore there is less structure on which to base world order today--NATO and CSCE, for example, have changed and we have yet to see if they remain effective in their new forms. The UN rapid response and co-ordination of multinational operations is inadequate at the moment. Furthermore, these multinational organizations have considerable difficulty gaining consensus in the post-Cold War era because of the huge differences between states and their agendas. The world's sole superpower, the US, has shown evidence recently of less resolve to intervene on behalf of international order. Many believe that there is a serious lack of statesmanlike leaders who might prevail in the event of further nastiness. Russia continues to be unstable and is showing some desire to recover some of her satellites, as well as her superpower status. The ruble has collapsed and Russians remain unpaid. With China flexing her muscles, India and Pakistan escalating the nuclear arms race, and other countries modernizing fast, the global power structure is shifting. Africa is beset with disease, overpopulation, crime, feeble or dictatorial governments, and religious extremism. Some nations, like Iraq and Libya, only understand the diplomacy of military might. Nuclear proliferation may have slowed but growth is inevitable--the development of nuclear programs in the Indian sub-continent (the most recent tests occurred in May 1998), Israel, and South Africa, and France's violations of the Non-Proliferation Treaty attest to that. The spread of advanced, non-nuclear weapon technologies, such as chemical and biological, and their delivery systems, are also inevitable. This type of modern warfare is available to less-developed nations who can exploit them in conflicts, leveling the playing field surprisingly quickly. Who then will guard the peace and with what, if terrorists get their hands on any of these weapons?

While all this is very sobering, there is also some cause for hope in a period devoid of superpower rivalry. There are large zones of peace and stability in Europe and North America and the nuclear threat has diminished. There is optimism for a newly effective global community through the UN--the opportunity in Eastern Europe, Russia, and Asia does exist. More nations like Australia, Pakistan and Malaysia are participating in UN peacekeeping efforts. There is more compassion towards human problems; democracy and capitalism are in the ascendant. Arms control continues; for example, over 7000 tanks belonging to former Warsaw Pact countries have been destroyed and START I and II ensure the elimination of multi-warhead ICBMs by 2003.[19] Mulling all this over, we can summarize that the threat of global war is lower today, but the world remains a singularly unpeaceful and highly volatile place.

Experts are having difficulty reading the messages from the former Soviet Union. Intelligence indicates that the navy is strong, modern and modernizing. Earlier in the decade, thirty-six submarines and forty-eight surface ships were scrapped--but all were obsolete and many had been in reserve. Ten submarines and nine major warships were launched following the break-up of the Warsaw Pact and more were laid down. The ballistic missile submarine force has remained intact but is apparently not growing. In 1995, the US reported the resumption of Russian hunter-killer patrols to monitor US ballistic missile submarine movements at their homeports on both coasts.

With the Soviets no longer the threat they were, whom should Canada consider her enemy? Well, we don't have one anymore in the direct military sense--at least not at the moment--and many experts feel that another opponent is unlikely to materialize directly against North America and NATO. This lack of a defined foe is one of the arguments that the peace lobby uses to press for deeper defence spending cuts and even disarmament. But additionally we have to ask, "Who's to know that another enemy won't pop up?" If we did disarm, it also means abandoning our obligations to the defence of North America, to our NATO-Europe allies, and to the victims of aggression abroad. To abandon just the latter would have Canadians in an uproar--it is part of our national persona to provide for the less fortunate. But improving the plight of the oppressed in this nasty world means having to have armed forces that are very well trained and equipped to conduct these vital humanitarian relief and peacekeeping missions in the midst of conflict.

There are several global flash points at the end of the century that materialized after the Cold War when political power vacuums resulted. The Department of National Defence includes the following in their list of potential trouble spots:

- The Asia-Pacific region, where power is developing like never before. Politics in China have evolved and are evolving since the passing of Mao Tse Tung, and with its huge population, the nation is feeling ever stronger. The region is becoming the driving force of the world economy, despite the recent collapse in the Asian stock markets, if only because of sheer numbers and the need to modernize in many countries. Canada is closely linked to the area with growing markets, many immigrants who have brought new skills and energy to us, and the Pacific fisheries.

- The northwest Pacific where Japan, China, Taiwan and the two Koreas are jostling for regional balance;

- Southeast Asia where the South China Sea's oil reserves incite bitter national rivalry. The hopes for cooperative security have decreased recently and the withdrawal of the US and Soviet Union from the region has left a vacuum that China yearns to fill. The SE Asian countries are strengthening their defence capability and now 35% of global arms procurement is made by these countries alone;

- The north Indian Ocean where Middle Eastern rivalries are interwoven with Indo-Pakistani disagreements and nuclear weapon testing;

- In the South Pacific where there is increasing international opposition to continued French nuclear testing and their imposition of an exclusion zone around the test area. In the future, opposition may entail more than visits from politicians. What if Japan sends a warship instead of their finance minister?

- In the Middle East where conflict is escalating and many direct their blame for terrorist activity.

- In Africa where anything goes;

- In the former Yugoslavia where the Serbs and Kosovars are unable to co-exist; and

- In Central and South America where politics and rivalries are always very unpredictable.

Only one thing is certain, we cannot predict anything--be it future centres of power or conflicts between nations or peoples. We must be prepared to do our duty--at home and as a global citizen--to the best of our ability. This is the only responsible attitude to adopt for the new millennium. However we do not need a clearly defined military threat to have a national security strategy--non-military threats require coordinated responses every bit as much as military threats. Threats still exist in peacetime-- they may be inactive or hidden, but they may also be very powerful. Weaker nations are often attractive to strong countries for economic or strategic reasons, or simply as a means to gain support for their policies, for example the Iraqi invasion of Kuwait. We cannot predict what pressure the stronger state will decide to exert on the weaker to achieve their ends, or who the players might be in the future. Distant states as well as neighbouring states can hanker after another's assets, especially when they have interests far afield left over from previous imperial glories.

Our own 1994 Defence White Paper sums it all up, "It is impossible to predict what will emerge from the current period of transition, but it is clear that we can expect pockets of chaos and instability that will threaten international peace and security."[20] Canada clearly anticipates having to do her duty to the world in the future and that means having the equipment and personnel to do it.

Maritime threats to nations are two-fold--they come at sea and by sea. A greedy nation can threaten maritime resources such as fisheries and oil and gas reserves, as well as shipping. Vessels at sea or oil platforms can be sabotaged, hijacked, get caught up in someone else's conflict, or be attacked by pirates. There is also the administrative threat--when another nation disputes ownership of land, boundaries, or maritime passages in international law. The presence of maritime forces often provides a strong diplomatic advantage in disputes of this kind. Interests that can be threatened from the sea include islands (the Falklands), mainland regions (often invaded by amphibious forces, like the D-day landings, during a war), and cities, which can be bombarded from the sea. To say that all of these threats are unlikely for Canada is clearly unrealistic--we have already faced one serious assault on our fisheries in this decade and have had several disputed islands and marine passages.

The threats to nations that come by sea, come via the shallow coastal waters surrounding the countries--submarines can move up the large rivers; they can sink shipping where it concentrates in the approaches to major ports; ships can carry troops for amphibious landings; and ships can bombard cities and shore installations. While not a serious threat to Canadian ports and cities at this time, all of these scenarios can and do take place around the world where the government sends Canadian ships and personnel. Coastal security is often inadequate and easily breached. It is not so easily reinstated.

Shallow waters surrounding coastal states remain the most difficult geophysical environments in which armed forces have to operate, and until fairly recently, were not the focus of the major navies of the world. Rock strewn bottom configurations, variable tidal currents, salinity and temperature differences, and the noise of heavy maritime traffic in littoral waters affect sonar. Detecting and classifying shallow underwater contacts is a nightmare and many potential operating areas have not been investigated. Furthermore, small powers often use mines to protect themselves from threats from the sea, as they are cheap and do not need warships to lay them. The ships and personnel necessary to counter this activity are out of all proportion to the threat, often tying up assets that could be used effectively elsewhere. Today most western navies are scrambling to enhance their shallow water knowledge and improve their operational capability in this most difficult of areas, Canada among them.

Make no mistake about it, countries cannot leave their defence preparedness until tricky situations become apparent. Threats to world stability can develop with little warning and with terrifying speed. The invasion of the Falkland Islands by Argentina in the early '80s and Iraq's invasion of Kuwait in 1990 are prime examples of just how fast things can happen even today. Satellite intelligence, assets on the ground, and analyses of local and regional politics did not fully predict what was going to happen and caught Britain, Kuwait, and their allies unprepared. These invasions occurred overnight, and unless defence preparedness had been adequate, could have prevailed. As it was the defenders-- Britain, in one case, and a UN coalition force in the other--did have the personnel and equipment to extricate the oppressed, but at some cost. Not only were the conflicts unforeseen, they also took place very far away from the nations who mounted the rescues.

Since then, we have seen the terrible civil wars in Kosovo, Bosnia, and Rwanda, where the racial strife exceeded everyone's worst imagination. NATO and UN forces had to go in and try not only to provide humanitarian aid on an enormous scale, but also to keep the warring factions apart at great peril to the troops. Canada was at sea, in the air, and on the ground in all theatres from the beginning.

One can only wonder what the next century will bring in the way of conflicts, disasters, and tension if the last few years have contained catastrophes such as these that needed armed resolution. We would be prudent to predict more of the same, however much we don't want to, and to be prepared to meet them.

Chapter Four
CANADA IS UNIQUE

anada is a country of paradoxes. It is small and yet big; it is
a continent and yet an island; it is rich and yet poor; it is
land and yet sea. These are some of the characteristics that
defence planners juggle when developing our policy and programs.
Let us try and put ourselves into their shoes.

Canada is a unique country in a unique position. This nation,
simply put, is HUUUUUUUGE and few Canadians realize just
how big this makes our defence requirements. Canada owns 9.976
million square kilometres of land (7% of the Earth's total landmass
and second in size only to Russia), which is surrounded by three
oceans. It is this geographical fact, which is of most interest to this
discussion--these oceans add 11 million square kilometres more of
both sovereign territory and areas of military responsibility to our
real estate holdings and they are some of the most inhospitable
waters on the planet. This area has been dubbed the "seaward"
Canada, and joining our land to our seas are 244,000 kilometers of
coastline, the longest in the world. Seven million Canadians, fully
one-quarter of the population, live in coastal areas of our country,
and only two provinces do not have a direct connection to the
ocean. Our prosperity is linked to the sea with fisheries, seabed

resources, and 40% of our GDP is derived from trade with others, mostly carried by sea.

The northern oceans that surround us are nasty and most unpredictable. The weather here can be brutal, with winds at storm force, waves higher than twenty meters and well below-freezing temperatures. One ocean is completely ice-covered throughout a very long and dark winter, and fog and icebergs abound in some areas. We also tend to forget that one of our most important sea lanes is also ice-bound in the winter--the Gulf of St. Lawrence. Additionally, the sound characteristics of the waters of our continental shelf are demanding, if not downright impossible sometimes. If this is not enough, our coasts are often lee shores, rocky and treacherous, with currents and winds that can force disabled vessels onshore all too easily.

The Arctic is another distinct component of this country (all 5.4 million sq. kms of it) and one that can never be forgotten in a defence context. Its characteristics bring a whole new collection of requirements if we are to assert our sovereignty up there, and its strategic value to Canada is critical. Canadians are fiercely proud of their northern heritage--we see the Arctic as ours. "The true north, strong and free" defines us as a nation and as a people, though few of us have ventured there for a look. However, the Arctic is not all ours however much we might like to think it is. Looking down on the world from above the North Pole, we see that Canada shares the Arctic frontier with the United States (Alaska), Norway, Denmark (Greenland), Iceland, Sweden, Finland, and Russia.

Certainly our Arctic territory is big--part of our continental landmass is above the Arctic Circle--and we have the longest Arctic shoreline of any NATO nation. It is a Canadian misconception, however, that our Arctic territory extends from the northern limits of our mainland to the North Pole.

At the end of the 1800s Canada declared that the Arctic Archipelago had been part of two previous British land transfers and included it in the District of Franklin when it was formed in the Northwest Territories. Since that time the Arctic islands have been considered Canadian and successive governments have operated under this interpretation. The initial lack of effective occupation and control up there, which nations traditionally and legally use to claim sovereignty, drew disputes from other countries in the early part of the 20th century. These forced Canada to establish permanent RCMP outposts there by 1922, but little was done to control the *waters* that we claimed were ours.

Even the launching of nuclear-powered submarines in the mid-fifties and the under-ice voyage of the USS *Nautilus* in August 1958, which changed the strategic value of the Arctic waters forever, did nothing to propel Canadian governments into taking action to protect this territory. The Arctic Archipelago is a mass of huge islands, myriad smaller ones, fjords, narrow straits, vast

Map 1 : The Arctic region viewed from above the North Pole

uninhabited areas, tiny settlements, and a fragile ecology. It is ice covered most of the year, suffers permanent darkness and permanent daylight, unbearably cold temperatures and howling blizzards. And yet it is most desirable territory. Within this vast array of islands, lie three of the world's ten largest islands, as well as the coveted North West Passage that joins the Pacific and the Atlantic Ocean. Little did the 19th century politicians realize the significance their claim would have on Canadian sovereignty and security in the latter half of the 20th century!

Disputes over our Arctic claims have not gone away, although there have been none concerning the Arctic landmass for more than sixty years. The Arctic waters are another matter. The most important and best-known dispute is over the North West Passage.

The United States believes that the North West Passage is an international waterway, while Canada claims it as inland waters. Canada does so because control of access to the Arctic provides us with a powerful lever to influence our defence relationships. Regrettably, we have been unable to exert that control due to inadequate attention to defence spending. Twice Americans have asserted their belief in freedom of navigation by sending ships through the North West Passage. On both occasions, the Canadian media created the erroneous notion that the US refused to ask our permission. In fact, the US notified us of their intentions, which is exactly what should happen from a Canadian point of view. Canada has always been involved with these US ventures--sending along observers aboard the US vessels and a Canadian Coast Guard icebreaker to help.

The tanker *Manhattan*'s and the US Coast Guard's *Polar Sea's* voyages through the North West Passage in 1969 and 1985 resulted in a storm of misplaced public protest due to the media's sensationalism and a series of Canadian political actions to attempt to exercise control over waters we claim as internal but are unable to patrol. We declared several extensions to our territorial limits in the hopes of ending the dispute but the Americans would not be moved. The 1990 Arctic Waters Pollution Prevention Act increased our jurisdiction over pollution control above 60 degrees north to 100 miles from land, but it was not recognized internationally, except by the then Soviets. Subsequent Canadian defence policies began to give protection of Canadian sovereignty more priority over collective security arrangements and culminated in 1987 with the newly elected Tory government's White Paper. This policy recognized and increased the strategic value of the Canadian Arctic by a quantum leap with the promise to acquire twelve nuclear-powered submarines for the three-ocean concept. With that, the Americans saw themselves as Canada's unnamed threat.[21] The dispute remains unresolved to this day, though in 1988 Canada and the US agreed to develop cooperative procedures to facilitate icebreaker navigation through the North West Passage. Not surprisingly, it did *not* extend to submarine operations in the Arctic but would have done if we had an underwater presence there.

Map 2: Northwest Passage (red) and submarine (blue) routes through the Arctic.

Canada's aspirations of exerting sovereignty in the Arctic to increase our voice in our defence relationships and becoming NATO's northern expert were never backed up with defence spending for adequate patrols or research. Any hope of doing so dissolved with the collapse of the Warsaw Pact and our economy. However we still look northward with intense longing. There are oil and gas reserves, significant and unique environmental concerns, fish stocks, and even growing tourism in the north, all of which should be of concern to Canadians.

Clearly our oceans and coastline go a long way to defining our nation. Water surrounds Canada on three sides and even our southern border with the US cuts through several of the Great Lakes. Only two other nations in the world have coastlines on three oceans--the United States and Russia. Canada's two coasts are separated by 11,000 kilometres of land and the third is ice covered most of the year. Our huge coastline is further divided into the 71,000 kilometres of the mainland shore and the 79,000 kilometres around our 52,455 islands. And some of our islands in the Pacific and Atlantic are bigger than countries--for example, Vancouver Island with Victoria, the capital of British Columbia, Newfoundland with St. John's, and Prince Edward Island. Yes, we truly are a huge maritime nation and our oceans have been likened to our "gates."

The immense, seaward Canada consists of all our maritime approaches, our territorial twelve nautical mile limit, our 200 nautical mile Exclusive Economic Zone (EEZ), our continental shelf, and our treaty-assigned ocean areas of responsibility, and it totals 11 million sq. kms. Canada is bound by the United Nations Convention on the Law of the Sea (UNCLOS), which governs all aspects of our ocean space, as well as that of other maritime nations. This international treaty covers the environmental control, marine scientific research, economic and commercial activities of the world's oceans and governs the settlement of disputes relating to ocean matters. UNCLOS states, amongst many other things, that coastal states have sovereignty over their territorial sea, their continental shelves, and their natural resources and certain economic activities in their EEZs. The Canadian EEZ covers 4.7 million square kilometers, and if you include internal Arctic waters, it covers just over 8 million. Canada's Oceans Act, proclaimed in early 1998 to clarify and streamline the management of our oceans, is based on the Law of the Sea's 320 articles. The act aims to integrate many of our fragmented agencies and programs of the past to ensure the harmonious and sustainable use of Canada's contiguous seas. The implication is immense--for the first time sea power, ocean development, and ocean management are in this together. This new approach brings with it tremendous opportunities as well as significant responsibilities to Canadians-- responsibilities of prudent management and protection of our EEZ's resources that the Department of National Defence (and other ministries) has to incorporate into its policy.

Environmental protection of the oceans is a fairly new concept. Historically, oceans have been the planet's garbage dump and it was not until relatively recently that the world started to realize the effects of this indiscriminate pollution. Despite the realization, the environmental risk around the world and in Canadian waters remains high. The need for double-hulled tankers is critical--only 8% have this design feature and only one of thirty-one Canadian tankers is so equipped. Canada experiences, on average, two hundred small accidental oil or chemical spills a year, ten medium spills and one major one. However the Department of National Defence, now responsible for ocean environmental protection, is only equipped to respond to small spills. In addition, the fragile Arctic maritime environment continues to require more research and responsible stewardship to protect it.

The ocean disasters of the 1980s have shifted the focus away from marine science and technology-based ocean development to a more regulatory approach. But even with this change, technology will still provide the means for conservation and protection of the oceans. For example, marine robotics, ocean information systems including mapping, and cold-ocean technologies are amongst the key areas for development in Canada.

Coastal states have sovereign rights over their continental shelves. They may explore them for minerals, oil, and gas, and having found deposits, may exploit them for national benefit. Fish, except for highly migratory species like salmon, also belong to the nation that owns the shelf. The shelves can extend at least 200 nautical miles from the shore and more under specified circumstances. Our immense continental shelf is the second largest in the world, covering 6.5 million square kilometers and has an additional margin outside of our EEZ of 1.8 million sq. kms. It is bigger off our Atlantic coast than the Pacific.

Canada's continental shelf contains some of the world's largest untapped reserves of offshore oil and natural gas that are of untold monetary value. The Scotia Shelf and Hibernia fields are already producing, with much more to come. The Beaufort Sea/Mackenzie Delta and the Arctic Islands also have proven crude oil reserves and 25% of our marketable natural gas reserves. We own extensive reserves of sand and gravel for construction, silica for solar cells and fibre optic cables, placer gold, and calcium carbonate for agriculture. Seawater itself is a source of lithium, deuterium, magnesium, iodine, sodium, and bromide. And while both the Atlantic cod and Pacific salmon fisheries are seriously depleted and in crisis, should they eventually recover, they will again present a significant economic resource to the nation. Our traditional fishing industry has employed as many as 90,000 Canadians and Canada was for many years the world's largest fish exporter--in 1988 the value of our fish exports was over $2.7 billion and in 1994 $2.8 billion, with the east coast contributing $1.8 billion. Many still hope we can be number one again. Meantime, our shellfish industry on both coasts is worth over $700 million annually and is growing rapidly.

Through our membership in NATO, Canada has a joint responsibility for even more ocean. The Canadian navy can be called upon to operate in an area in the north Atlantic stretching from Labrador to Greenland, south to the mid-Atlantic and from there, west to Nova Scotia, either alone or in company with other NATO navies. When added to our Atlantic territorial responsibilities of 2 million sq. km. this area increases our total to 3.7 million sq. km. In the north Pacific, Canada is responsible for 1.9 million sq. km., which includes the 380,000 sq. km. of the approaches to the Juan de Fuca Strait and the approaches to northern BC waters, as well as 27,000 km. of coastline. While we share some of the responsibility for the seaward approaches with the US, this does not absolve Canada of our sovereign obligations. While not all these zones require sovereignty protection, they do demand a significant obligation from this country to our allies through the Department of National Defence and the navy.

The sea has been and still is a vital factor in Canada's economy--much of our industry depends on a sustained flow of exports and imports, most of which are moved by sea. For example, Eastern Canada is completely dependent on imported oil for the time being, which makes us vulnerable to disruptions in oil supply or in the ocean routes over which the oil must travel. Likewise, our ability to export can be influenced by any event that affects our trading partners--be it insurrection or a natural disaster.

Ocean industries and shipborne trade accounted for 36.6% of Canada's gross domestic product (in 1995) and 30% of our gross national product comes from international trade, 55% of which travels by sea. Annually, our twenty-five deep-water ports and 650 smaller ports handle more than 350 million tonnes of seaborne trade. The great Atlantic and Pacific ports, the Cabot Strait, the St. Lawrence Seaway, the Great Lakes, and the Strait of Juan de Fuca are the marine arteries that make us prosper. Vancouver, for example, is the second busiest port in North America in terms of cargo handled and reflects the importance of the Pacific Rim to us. This seaborne trade accounts for over 52,000 individual ship loadings and unloadings per year--29,532 in international trade alone and almost as many, 23,108, in domestic trade. There is a substantial network of coastal shipping that supports our more isolated communities, as well as our growing offshore resource industry. We also need to remember that 25% of US-bound oil goes by sea from Valdez, Alaska, to the continental US through the Canadian area of responsibility in the Pacific.

There can be no doubt that the use of the world's oceans will increase in scope and complexity in the next century and this cannot help but have implications for the world and Canada. What they will be, we can only guess. Certainly some of the implications will have a direct impact on Canadian security and the Department of National Defence will have to respond, integrating the policy with the tools. The Canadian navy will be front and centre in meeting the challenges of law enforcement, marine emergencies, and protection of maritime sovereignty, alongside the Canadian Coast Guard and the Department of Fisheries and Oceans.[22] Surveillance of our huge seaward Canada will take all of our presently slim resources of air, surface and sub-surface assets and then some.

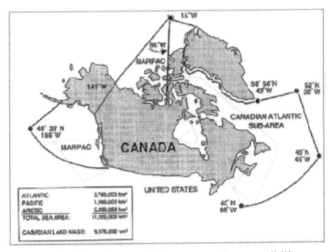

Map 3: Canadian maritime areas of responsibility.
(Fine lines show fishing grounds)

Not only must Canadians and our defence planners look at Canada's geographical position and scope, we must also examine Canada's position in the world. Where do we fit in with our neighbours, our allies, and non-aligned nations? Are we welcome at the tables of power and the world's councils? Do we have any influence? How do others see us?

Canada's position at the top of North America is an interesting one geopolitically. The continent is in between the powerful Asia-Pacific and Europe-Atlantic regions with the US overpowering the other smaller nations within the landmass. An American observer wrote that the USA perceives that her northern (Canada) and southern neighbours (Central America and the Caribbean) are a weak link in the continental power structure.[23] The US will always pursue its own interests--apart from the strong military ties, there is little of the "special" relationship with Canada that politicians on both sides of the border would have us believe in.

Our friends are mostly western industrialized nations and our closest neighbour and ally is the world's sole remaining superpower. However it is important to remember that lesser nations are always attractive to a super power for economic and strategic reasons, to say nothing of support for their policies. Whether we like it or not, a threat to the US is a threat to us due to our geographic attachment to them. Canada also needs to remain vigilant in safeguarding our interests, from culture to defence. If we choose specifically to neglect our own defence, partially or completely, the US would likely feel compelled to fill the vacuum. By letting it happen, we could forfeit our sovereignty. Thus, keeping our ability to protect our sovereignty is very important to retaining our credibility with the US as an independent nation--the Americans respect those who look after themselves.

We are also one of Britain's closest friends, and as a founding and active member of NATO, we feel close to Europe. However, Europeans do not reciprocate those feelings to Canada as much as they do towards the US. Canadians are somehow lumped in with Americans in this context. As a member of the Commonwealth we have other friends all over the globe and feel strong ties with the other former British colonies of Australia and New Zealand. We are working at developing relationships in the Asia-Pacific region, some of which are coming to fruition.

Others see us in a variety of ways--some good, some not so good. Many have-not countries envy Canada, especially since we led the list of countries deemed "best to live in" by the UN. Occasionally Britain's actions remind us that they see us as a colony which is still growing up, that needs to be led by the hand in some areas, and at times defence is one of them. Our reputation with NATO is one of a nation that never pulls its weight; that has never fully contributed. The UN sees us as always being ready, willing, and able to provide forces for peace-keeping, however dangerous the mission. Countries and defence contractors who try to sell us equipment, like helicopters and submarines, think Canada is a high-risk customer--they can never be certain that Canada will see the big defence contracts through to completion.

Canadians know we are definitely not a super-power, but what exactly are we? We have the physical size of a major power, we are a member of the Group of Seven[*] (G7), now known as G8 with the addition of Russia as a member, and we are a founding member of NATO. But we have a small military, a big national debt, and a small population.

"Super power" is wielded not only by size and population, but also by economy, political influence, cultural, military, intellectual, and perceived world position. It is a characteristic of nations with the resources to protect all their interests, near and far, and who believe that no problem in the world can be solved without their intervention. They have a stake in peace and freedom everywhere and know if their economies weaken or collapse, there will be serious repercussions around the world.

Other nations, by contrast, do not wield that level of influence or, dare we say it, arrogance. But when they demonstrate that they are in charge of their own destinies and have some independent means to maintain their national identity and interests, we classify them as a medium power. Medium powers can also be identified by their inability to protect everything they own or defend themselves alone, the maintenance of their initiative for safeguarding their interests, and by their formation of alliances, preferably with a super power. They also look to their allies for help when necessary, but are realistic enough to realize they cannot always rely on their assistance for all the crises they might face. A medium maritime power will aim to use the sea to enhance its autonomy and power--how strategy. It is important for nations like Canada to balance their defence strategy. For example, for Canada to deploy the navy predominately on multinational operations overseas weakens our ability to protect our sovereignty and our own interests at sea, as well as our capacity to promote ourselves by the sea.

On close examination, Canada fits the criteria of a medium power, but unlike many in this category, has immense maritime responsibilities to contend with--a profile filled with contradictions and inherent planning difficulties. Super, medium, and small maritime powers have different types of navies, which are suited to their domestic needs, foreign policies, and available funds. They fall into four categories:

---

*The Group of Seven (eight if we include Russia) refers to the seven leading industrialized nations

1. Global navies have balanced fleets containing their own air and amphibious branches with world-wide interests and reach (e.g. USA);

2. Ocean-going navies have interests in distant waters and the capability to carry out a single unsupported major operation against all but the most sophisticated opponent (e.g. UK and France);

3. Contiguous sea or regional navies have some capability to operate beyond their contiguous seas, normally as part of an alliance (e.g. Germany, Holland, and Canada); and,

4. Coastal or territorial defence navies are limited to operating within their EEZs (e.g. Norway and Denmark).[24]

The Canadian navy fits into the third category, regional, like most navies from the developed world, but faces very different challenges than a Germany or Holland. Our enormous maritime territory with its extensive Arctic component and abundant ocean resources requires more vessels, often of a different type, than most nations in this category. Furthermore, we have, since about 1949, tended to specialize in ASW, and have subordinated our national requirements to alliance needs and our reliance on NATO.

Financial strictures are the last, but not the least, ingredient defence planners have to take into consideration. Even though Canada is a member of the G8 and has to protect our vast land, sea and air space, our military is ranked only 55th in size in the world and our defence spending, as a percentage of our GDP, is ranked 114th. This is partly caused by our population* of nearly 30 million--our tax base is small and our debt has become large. In addition, successive governments have postponed or denied regular improvement of defence equipment and have not provided sufficient funds to meet our domestic and international security

*Canada's population ranks 50th in the world.

responsibilities. For the navy, this meant a lot of making do until the new frigates and Maritime Coastal Defence Vessels (MCDV) came on stream, with too few ships and submarines, reduced personnel, and outdated equipment. This situation resulted in the navy's difficulty in pulling its weight in domestic and overseas obligations. For the submarine squadron it meant not having a boat on the west coast despite the growing importance of the Asia-Pacific region, reduced operational readiness, and mounting fears until April 1998 that the Canadian Submarine Service would be disbanded.

Canada ranks 13th of fifteen NATO nations in defence spending, but has by far the largest ocean territory to protect. Between 1994 and 1999, Canada's poor fiscal position, led to deep cuts in defence spending--the Department of National Defence made reductions in both military and civilian personnel government to make (33% by 1999), in support services, and in infrastructure, so that those who go in harm's way could be more adequately equipped. But despite that stated objective, capital expenditure was also reduced by $1 billion/year for fifteen years. With no choice in the matter, DND had to place the emphasis on the acquisition of equipment considered essential to the core capability of the CF.

The unspoken message here for the public is that governments can target defence spending for ruthless cuts without damaging our security or our economy.[25] Just looking at the responsibilities that governments apportion to the Department of National Defence, it is clear that cuts would have serious repercussions on all sorts of services to the nation, to our allies, and to peacekeeping. Other myths,[26] which have rarely been refuted by governments or the popular press, are that defence spending is a major cause of Canada's federal debt and that cutting defence costs will somehow solve the nation's financial predicament. Today defence spending accounts for only 7.4% of the federal budget, so even if you got rid of it entirely it wouldn't help the debt significantly. To put this in other ways--since 1962 defence costs, as a percentage of total government expenditures, have dropped over 71%, while other expenditures have risen 30%; and Canada now spends over five times more on debt servicing each year than it does on national security. Clearly, defence is not a cause of the federal debt.[27]

Defence program planners have to meet the government's taskings, the responsibilities of huge land and sea areas, and the directive to do it all with what amounts to a couple of bucks. "Our goals are to continue providing Canada with an affordable and effective multi-purpose, combat-capable force, while at the same time doing our part to help in the fight against the deficit," said the Honourable David Collenette, when he was the minister of national defence. Not an easy task.

Chapter Five
CANADA'S PREPAREDNESS

"Let him who desires peace, prepare for war."
Vegetius, circa 500AD

W hile foreign policy can change rapidly, overnight even, and still remain effective, defence policy cannot move that fast because it has personnel and equipment attached to it. It takes five or ten years for a major change in policy to be fulfilled if it requires new equipment and training. With overnight fixes impossible, defence planners have to prepare for probabilities and possibilities, often spanning decades. They are responsible for the two-pronged approach to defence planning-- first, developing the policy and second, designing programs to implement that policy within the government's budget allowances. Program planning, like business planning, focuses mainly on the department's expenditure plans which include personnel, operations and maintenance, and capital acquisitions over the medium and short term.

The current defence policy says, "A country of Canada's size and means cannot, and should not, attempt to cover the entire military spectrum, but the Canadian Forces must be able to make a genuine contribution to a wide variety of domestic and international objectives."[28] This statement puts Canada squarely into the category of needing a regional navy that can operate abroad as well as in our adjacent seas. It also infers that any major military equipment must serve a wide range of military and even, occasionally, civilian purposes. However, it is also important to realize that at the beginning of the 21st century the CF cannot get more effective by getting smaller.

It is well known that medium powers face significant challenges in defence preparedness and a country like Canada faces one of the greatest. We cannot do everything, but what can we safely *not* do? What *must* we do? Are there any compromises to be found? Our huge ocean "reach"--not for current international interests but simply for our own domestic security--our immense maritime areas, and our small population just add to our planning difficulties. Top it all up with Canada's money shortage and the program planning process becomes nightmarish.

Medium maritime powers like Canada must first answer two questions. What is the highest level of conflict we are prepared to engage in? What "reach" will our navy need to create a presence in areas of interest or to collectively engage a rogue regime? We must consider not only at what level we will respond to future threats but also how effective other measures, which we could employ to defuse them, might be

Canadian defence planners work on the basis of three levels of conflict:

1. **Peace** - a state of balanced tensions. Naval taskings include search and rescue, disaster relief, humanitarian assistance, surveillance and control of Canadian territory, which includes drug and illegal immigrants interdiction and counter-terrorism, evacuation of Canadians overseas, peace support operations such as maintaining a cease-fire, and aid of the civil power.

2. **Conflict** - these are active, organized hostilities involving opposing sides who use weapons but are limited in aim, scope, and area. Their aim is always clearly stated in military terms: e.g. "Recapture the

Falklands" and the rules of engagement are clear. More often than not, these operations are conducted in company with other friendly nations but can be managed alone by larger navies. For Canada this level embraces operations like the Gulf War and the defence of North American territory. Conflicts can be low, medium or high intensity.

3. **War** - this is the highest level of conflict and consumes the energies of whole countries--their civilian effort as well as their military. It holds the risk of escalation to nuclear warfare. For Canada, war would be fought in a collective defence scenario.

With the sole remaining superpower as an ally of ours, Canada probably can safely conclude that we will not have to provide a military response in a high-level conflict or general war in the near future. However, it is also safe to assume we will be required to engage with others in medium and low intensity regional wars around the world. If we are going to be engaged in low level conflicts overseas against small powers, Canada's navy can be frigate-sized with helicopters and a modest anti-submarine capability, without the necessary air cover because we can expect our allies to provide it. However if Canadian governments continue to choose to send our navy and personnel to the four corners of the globe on major coalition operations, like the Gulf War, the level of conflict can, and sometimes does, escalate rapidly. For this reason, planners lean towards ships that can defend themselves from attack from above and beneath the sea--and these tend to be very costly, much to the chagrin of the bean counters. One thing we all agree on is that all Canadians want their troops to have adequate equipment and protection when employed with multinational forces.

These expeditions also raise the issue of ocean "reach." Just how far away is the government likely to send our naval forces to promote peace around the world? The answer is probably anywhere, so our ships need to have very long range indeed. However, in Canada's case our navy must have long legs anyway for domestic reasons, so planners know this requirement is already a given. For most medium powers however, this huge "reach" requirement is unusual--with India and Australia being exceptions similar to Canada. Fleets that deploy far from home need to have specialized support systems and equipment on board, replenishment ships, and a high degree of self-sufficiency--all of which increase cost. The vessels' sea-keeping ability must also be borne in mind and designed for their likely operating areas. In Canada's case, our ships have to be excellent sea keepers anyway because of the inhospitable nature of our northern seas. Finally, planners know that you need three vessels to keep one on station, whether at home or overseas.

This discussion now leads us to our alliances. As we do not get collective protection for nothing, planners also have to look at what Canada can realistically offer our allies in return. Sometimes it can be geographical position, sometimes it is the offer of shared facilities, like Australia's VLF station which the US uses to communicate with her submarines, or it can be skills or raw materials. The US cultivation of Saudi Arabia as an ally for its oil is a prime example of the latter. However, for medium powers it is more often the offer of military forces. Canada provides a unique geographic position to our allies, as well as personnel and equipment. We have a ship permanently attached to NATO's Standing Naval Force Atlantic, for example, and personnel serving in NATO, NORAD, and several other allied headquarters.

Finally, planners have to look close to home. International law demands that to establish sovereignty a nation must be capable of monitoring activity in its nationally claimed areas. Sovereignty protection of a nation's economic zone is customarily a role for constabulary (law enforcement) forces, rather than for the sophisticated vessels and aircraft designed for medium to high intensity engagements which may take place thousands of miles away. However, any medium power with a long coastline and a big EEZ needs more than a maritime police force. They must have air and more powerful surface forces to gain the oceanic "reach" to operate at least to the limits of their EEZ, and must also have submarines.[29] If a country expects to use the same platforms for both policing and military functions, and many do, the coastal forces may end up being more sophisticated than necessary and may occasionally sail away with multinational forces to quell uprisings in other parts of the world. When this happens it sometimes creates the impression of "overkill"--frigates policing scallop fishers or submarines catching drug traffickers--but it is a more cost-effective solution than having two distinct fleets--one civilian and one military. Canada's defence policy also shows us that our government has decided that our armed services must be able to engage in low to moderate level conflicts anywhere on the planet and need to be able to protect the economic zones in our three oceans.

Once Canada's program planners have taken all the above factors into consideration, remembered the lessons of history (this is known in defence-babble as contingency-based planning), and have made some decisions, the navy ends up with a list of what it requires to do its job--the "force requirement." Next, the planners evaluate the assets the navy already has, consider if they are still suitable, or if they need upgrading, and how many years they have left in them. The gaps in the inventory translate into the programs that need implementing if the navy is uphold the government policy for the next five, ten, twenty years and so on. The government of the day then looks at the proposals and decides which, if any, they will support and pay for and when. In Canada, this is all too often where the policy and the programs part company and the navy is left with huge performance expectations and insufficient ships, equipment, and personnel with which to accomplish them.

The lack of a traditional enemy and the unpredictability of future world co-existence have made it very difficult for western defence planners to prepare for war or peace since the end of the 1980s. The surprise and the speed with which threats develop and escalate to serious conflicts emerge far faster than ships can be built or personnel can be trained. The Gulf and Falklands Wars are prime examples of the volatility that all planners face, however fiscal restraints have prevented the luxury of all-singing, all-dancing navies and have forced our Department of National Defence to prioritize ruthlessly. However, it is all too easy to get the plan wrong today and wishful thinking can lead us astray as well--the "If we don't have armed forces, we won't have to go to war" passive-aggressive attitude of the peace lobby. If it were that simple, war and the need for peacekeeping operations would not exist.

Canada certainly cannot afford, and probably does not need, every component of naval capability--in the past we have progressively divested ourselves of several specific naval platforms such as aircraft carriers and minesweepers, as well as the capabilities and expertise that went along with them. What else can the cash strapped planners scrap? Not much more, given the government's 1994 White Paper on Defence.

At the beginning of the twenty-first century, any naval policy that requires major program changes takes a bucketful of money and about a decade to bring to fruition. Getting rid of a capability does not and is a tempting route to follow in times of tight money. However, the danger in axing any branch of the navy is that it might well be needed and the decision has to be taken with immense caution. If the government had decided to discontinue our submarine branch, Canadians need to understand that the navy would not have been able to nip down to the corner store and buy a squadron of submarines off the shelf, to say nothing of developing the highly skilled and trained crews over a weekend, should the need arise. Therefore, the submarine decision, which Canada faced at the dawning of a new millennium, was a most critical one.

Chapter Six
CANADA NEEDS A NAVY

*"Navies are beginning to look
increasingly attractive."*[30]

C anada does not see itself as a maritime nation. But it is.
Canadians do not see that we have interests overseas. But
we do. Canadians do not see why we should have a navy.
But we must. It is easy and fashionable to base the need and make-
up of our navy solely on the frequency of our government's calls
for maritime peacekeeping abroad but this is not worthy of our
great nation at home. It fails to recognize the whole story and, most
importantly, the priority of our domestic need for a modern,
professional navy. Navies do not "just fight."

Canada's defence policy shows us that which we hold dear is
worth protecting and it tells us, in broad terms, what in the way of
armed services we need to implement it. Our sovereignty, our
geography, our jurisdictions, and our alliances, all define why we
need our navy and the form it should take. Experts expect
governments to become increasingly reliant on navies in the 21st
century as instruments of sovereignty protection, preventative
diplomacy, and maritime crisis management.

Canadians should find nearly 11,000,000 sq. kms. of ocean real estate and nearly 250,000 kilometers of coastline to monitor and safeguard sufficient reason to support the need for a navy at home, to say nothing of the character of our three oceans and the resources they provide. Add to that our huge reliance on seaborne trade--it is the greatest of all the G8 nations--and it is hard to understand why anyone questions the need for Canada to have a capable maritime force. Our navy legitimizes our maritime territory, protects our sovereignty and resources, provides law enforcement at sea, and saves lives in a very unforgiving environment. To be sovereign at sea, international law requires Canada to be able to control every activity in our area of jurisdiction on, above, and under the sea. To be anything less means that anyone can use our waters to do whatever they feel like, without regard for law.

Looking further afield, we share a continent and a relationship with the world's remaining superpower, with whom we cooperate to ensure continental stability but whom we regard with considerable caution. Yet Canada's interests are also linked through trade to global stability and require us to be engaged politically, diplomatically, and sometimes militarily around the world. As we are limited in the influence we can exert on world affairs by ourselves, due to our small population and isolation, we have sought multilateral solutions to world problems through NATO, OAS, the UN, APEC, and CSCE, to name a few organizations. These memberships have brought with them not only reassurance, but also obligations--defence related obligations. The continuing world disorder carries with it a worrying increase in regional conflicts that seriously threaten stability, and Canada has become involved with many of them, as she is a global citizen. All this and the surge of importance in the Pacific region over the last forty years just confirms how inextricably Canada is bound to the lives of others around the world. Our navy protects, and if necessary rescues, those less fortunate in distant lands because we are stable nation ourselves and have a reliable and professional navy.

One of the strengths of maritime forces lies in their immediate availability to respond to events domestically and internationally. Navies have participated in the resolution of many crises since WWII with government leaders and military commanders able to quickly configure naval responses to provide myriad options, both in peacetime and war. Navies can operate in forward areas with limited support and are much less constrained by political borders than armies and air forces, due to the right of innocent passage.

It is instructive here, when establishing why Canada needs a navy, to consider how the roles of our navy have evolved. In both world wars and through the Cold War, the dominant maritime role (80%) for the Canadian forces was protection of the sea-lanes across the North Atlantic against attack by submarines. Today this traditional focus has shifted dramatically and our navy spends 75% of its time undertaking the following:

- surveillance and control of Canadian territory, including ocean resource management, maintenance of the maritime environment, and the maintenance of law and order at sea;

- participation in bi- or multilateral operations directly related to national and international security;

- provision of emergency and humanitarian relief, including search and rescue;

- assistance to and/or support of other government departments; and

- response to requests for aid of the civil power.[31]

Several of these roles use a navy's traditional function of sea control, which has not changed for centuries. The increased emphasis on sovereignty protection has occurred not only because the Cold War ended, but also because of increasing numbers of challenges to our territory and our resources. Furthermore, the navy's shift away from protection of shipping by no means diminishes the importance of anti-submarine warfare skills as many have construed--we will find out why this is in the next chapter.

The **surveillance and control** role, which also encompasses law enforcement, is arguably the most important for Canada at the turn of the century. The Canadian navy is no stranger to this role.

We have had increasing challenges in this area in the 1980's and 1990's--resource depletion, pollution, illegal immigration, and criminal activity--all of which have enlarged the scope of our domestic maritime operations--and all of which show little sign of abating. Detecting and monitoring this type of activity in our vast maritime territory is our "keystone of sovereignty."[32] It also involves protection of resources and personnel through application of laws and regulations, upholding our position over boundary lines and the straits issues in the Arctic and elsewhere, and prevention of illegal activities.

It may come as a surprise to Canadians that we have some territory to look after which is disputed by the US, Denmark and, until recently, France. The Americans believe the Northwest Passage in the Arctic is an international strait, but since 1985, Canada has claimed all of the Arctic Archipelago as internal waters. The Beaufort Sea and Machias Seal Island in the Bay of Fundy are other points of disagreement between our neighbour and ourselves.

As recently as this decade, Dixon Entrance, a US/Canadian strait near Prince Rupert just north of the Queen Charlotte Islands in BC, led to a dispute(see map overleaf). Canada believed that USN nuclear-powered submarines were using our waters of Dixon Entrance when proceeding to and from their Alaska support facility and we sought a mechanism by which the Americans would seek permission every time they wanted to make the passage. Eventually an agreement was made that the USN would simply notify us of their intentions, but the whole affair caused Canada to lose some face--if we had been operating submarines in the Pacific, Canada would have been getting that information automatically as a fellow submarine operator.

Denmark claims an island between Greenland and Ellesmere Island as hers and in 1992 the World Court ruled on the boundary around the French islands of Saint-Pierre and Miquelon, south of Newfoundland. The boundary dispute was settled but the ensuing requirement of both countries to jointly manage the fishery is causing some difficulties.

**Map 4: The northwestern British Columbia
coast showing Dixon Entrance.**

Only stable nations can participate in **bilateral and
multilateral operations** in this unpredictable world. Often thought
of as the "business of soldiers," peacekeeping is primarily a
combined operation of the most complicated type. Maritime
peacekeeping can include sea control, surveillance, preservation or
restoration of order at sea, and sealift and logistic support,
sometimes in distant and violent places. Navies have tremendous
utility in this type of role. For example, ships do not need land
bases to support them; they can provide government with a wide
range of options from sanctions to multi-threat warfare; they can
respond fast to national policy direction; and lastly they all have
outstanding command, control, and communications. Only
professional navies can undertake this type of work and the
Canadian navy has always been one of these. Maritime
peacekeeping is neither a new idea nor is it an artificial invention
to justify having a navy after the Cold War as some commentators

would have us believe. Modern naval peacekeepers perform the same tasks that sailing ships did in previous centuries.

Navies regularly provide warships, contingents of naval personnel, and skilled individuals to maritime peacekeeping forces. In almost every major peacekeeping mission Canada has been involved in, our naval vessels have participated--often having been the first assets arrive at the scene. In other examples, we sent thirty naval personnel to Cambodia as observers on their rivers, lakes and coast and Canada provided divers, harbourmasters, and vessel traffic management personnel to several other multilateral efforts.

The surveillance role and multilateral operations always involve control of the sea, though to differing degrees. In its most simplistic definition, sea control prevents the illegal or unauthorized use of a specific part of the ocean. It is achieved in various ways--monitoring large areas of ocean for sovereignty reasons and resource management, verifying the compliance of others with international agreements, enforcing economic sanctions or arms embargoes, or conducting search and seizure operations. Fisheries patrols are an example of domestic sea control for resource management and sovereignty purposes. NATO's operations in the Adriatic and the UN-sponsored activity in the Persian Gulf and off Haiti are classic examples of multilateral sea control used to prevent more arms feeding already violent conflicts.

However sea control mostly revolves around trade--either commodities being carried by sea or resources obtained from the sea. For centuries, world trade has been conducted by sea and this is still largely true today, though the tonnage and monetary worth of the cargoes have soared. It is all too easy for a rogue regime to hold the world hostage by closing a sea route that passes through restricted waters like the Straits of Hormuz in the Middle East (likely) or the Straits of Juan de Fuca (unlikely); by sinking cargo ships on the high seas as in WWII; or by denying access to ports. Most countries would be affected by actions such as these, but some would always be affected more than others, depending on the commodities and ports involved. The growth of super-ports around the world, like Rotterdam and Singapore, can make those countries or regions that depend on them, vulnerable to trade interruptions unless they have alternative ports of entry. While historically nations protected merchant ships under their national flag, today most trade is carried under flags of convenience. There is no agreement as to who is responsible for *their* protection, although in the cases of humanitarian aid, and perhaps care of refugees, there is an emerging collective responsibility. So it is in Canada's, and everyone else's, economic interest to see that trade continues unmolested--and this means controlling the sea in times of both peace and conflict. With the decline of major traditional maritime powers and the increase in international trade, trade assumes a place of high priority in anyone's security arrangements.

Sea control also applies to maritime areas of responsibility. These areas increased after the 1982 UN Law of the Sea Convention gave coastal states the right to administer resources within their 200 nautical mile economic zones and several disputes arose, some of which are still unresolved. The value of the resources in the disputed areas are usually at the root of any potential confrontations and the possibility always exists that nations might take the solution into their own hands or a multilateral coalition might respond for the common good. Thus, maritime boundaries at home and abroad become a security issue for Canada, and a job of sea control for our navy. At home, sea control prevents our sovereignty and security from violation and is best met by having submarines, ships, and patrol aircraft monitoring activity in all dimensions of our ocean areas.

The UN Law of the Sea may be a superb legal entity, but there is no international mechanism for enforcement. As international demands grow ever louder, the world's politicians will inevitably look to navies to conduct the surveillance and enforcement components (sea control) of the Law of the Sea because no other entity can do it. No doubt Canada and Canada's navy will be in the forefront.

Evidence shows that the Law of the Sea is being contravened increasingly these days. Illegal immigration, poaching of resources, drug running, piracy, dumping of pollutants, and smuggling are increasingly beyond the capabilities of most nations' agencies tasked with their control. If a fishing vessel is caught violating Canada's laws, something can be done if its country of origin has entered international agreements in good faith. But if the boat is flying a flag of convenience, what then? Who does Canada negotiate with? It is the navies of the world that provide most of the control now, and in the future, will do so increasingly.

Illegal drugs pour into North America by sea despite massive efforts to prevent them. Sea control is a very large part of a successful battle against narcotics entry and often has to be done in very isolated coastal areas. This is a job for the navy too, hand in hand with the Coast Guard and the RCMP. International terrorism is rising and there are hundreds of acts of piracy every year in South East Asia, the Caribbean, and the Mediterranean. Western navies are increasingly aware of their responsibilities should an incident occur on their watch and in their area.

Sea control has three essential components--surveillance, patrol, and response; in addition, Canada needs ocean reach. "Surveillance" means the systematic observation of our areas of maritime responsibility with the aim of detecting activity on, under, or above the sea. "Patrol" is the physical presence of a naval unit on, under, or above the ocean. And "response" is the ability to protect national interests in a timely manner wherever and whenever they are threatened. It is only the level of response that differentiates between the law enforcement and military roles of navies. The military response infers that force might have to be used, while law enforcement relies more on gathering evidence and the threat of court action. The three components of sea control for law enforcement or military tasks can only be achieved with sea power--and that means ships, aircraft, and submarines.

Sea power has evolved in its meaning and method since the era of huge fleets engaging each other in a "clash of titans" as occurred at the Battle of Jutland. The term was usually understood to mean the ability of a country to control the seas and project power across the ocean. Peter Haydon, a defence commentator, explains sea power in more modern Canadian terms, "If a state is dependent on the oceans or a particular part of an ocean for national security, then it makes sense that it be able to determine what happens in those waters. And these can be distant as well as home waters."[33] Put in less powerful terms maybe, but the statement still acknowledges that unless there is a fundamental change in human nature, the need to control the seas remains and will always remain to maintain order in our world. From a global perspective "...Sea power [is now] mainly concerned with the maritime dimension of problem-solving...where collective response is preferred to unilateral action"[34] to prevent rogues holding the world to ransom. Whether Canada should attempt to participate in all collective responses is, or should be, questionable. We need to choose those operations that we can afford and that are unlikely to escalate to a level for which our ships are neither designed nor prepared.

Naval forces, of course, are the instruments that provide sea power for both state and collective security requirements, ensuring security, sovereignty at sea, and support of foreign policies and overseas trade. Warships deploy quickly and independently, are flexible, and are legal extensions of their parent state. Their presence automatically implies the concern of their nation about a developing situation. This is true for Canada as well as for every other nation and ship deployment can be used for good or evil. We like to think we use it for good--our own and that of our allies, as well as for the oppressed. Just as the definition has broadened during this century, so have the skills required to provide sea power. Warships are now used to not only fight seaborne opponents, but also to collect, analyse, correlate and report data-- knowledge is power--as the saying goes. Today, information management is as accepted in diplomacy as it once was in responding to crises.

Sea power has also changed as the capabilities of warships have changed. These days naval vessels are much more capable than they used to be and navies have decreased in size because of it. Once measured in numbers of ships and weapons, sea power today is measured by the size of the ocean area a nation's navy can control. With a few modern ships, it is conceivable that a limited naval power could quickly seize a country or region before anyone else could come to their aid. That being so, it behooves us to consider which nations have augmented their naval capabilities in the last decade of the 20th century and it comes as no surprise that they are the same nations involved in the hot spots of the world discussed in Chapter Three. Indonesia, Malaysia, Singapore and Thailand are all expanding their maritime forces and both Koreas and Taiwan are rapidly modernizing. China is also on the naval bandwagon--once primarily having a coastal defence strategy, they are now pushing the envelope out further with a large maritime security zone and more capable naval platforms. The dispute of jurisdiction in the South China Sea is one reason for the flurry of activity. South Korea and Taiwan, of course, have clearly defined national threats to explain their build-ups. Admiral Bruce Johnston was in Malaysia in 1995 and wrote, "...there will be a crisis somewhere [in the Asia-Pacific region and] Canada and the Canadian Forces will be involved at some level."[35] Johnston believes the navy, and submarines along with it, is the only service that can make a meaningful contribution in the Pacific in the 21st century. Then there was Pakistan's nuclear sabre rattling in 1998 which explains why India presses on with its navy even though it has more capability than any neighbouring state. Equally worrisome is Iran with its new submarine service of three second-hand Russian Kilos, presumably to more effectively threaten forces in the gulf that are likely to seek their compliance with UN directives. Russia pleads penury but still deploys ships and submarines into the Atlantic and Pacific to shadow US surface and submarine forces. Although not expanding, the Russian navy is still very much alive and functioning, and no doubt will be used to further its interests.

Nor is sea power a relic of the past. Navies remain just as essential in the present and for the future--especially those designed and trained to work together like the Canadian and United States Navies. They are the forces of choice for politicians for sovereignty protection, diplomacy, and maritime crises around the world. This latter is borne out historically in Canada--our navy has often been the first of our armed services to be sent abroad in response to any international crisis. It happened in 1950 for Korea, in 1956 during the Suez Canal crisis, and in 1990 to the Persian Gulf.

Canadians take **emergency and humanitarian relief** seriously. Ships at sea have traditionally responded to emergencies regardless of the nationality of those in distress and the Canadian navy is no exception to this unwritten rule. However, their search and rescue (SAR) role is more formalized with the Canadian military co-ordinating the efforts on land and at sea from Halifax and Victoria. Disasters at sea require courageous, determined, and highly skilled interventions, for they rarely occur in calm, warm waters and our navy is proud to be involved, having the vessels, helicopters, and trained personnel who can handle the extreme dangers. In 1998, the loss of Swissair flight 111 off Peggy's Cove in Nova Scotia used ships, our submarine *Okanagan*, submersibles, and divers from the navy, as well as Canadian soldiers, to complete the recovery operation after authorities determined that rescue was impossible. Although not part of SAR, warships also provide comfort and relief in times of other types of disasters, often very quickly. The Canadian navy's arrival in Florida after Hurricane Andrew is a good example and it would do the same thing at home if needed by coastal communities. Ships provide moveable bases and an immediate sense of security to the victims in a way no other type of vessel can. They also represent authority and bring motivated personnel with a huge variety of skills who can be sent ashore to help survivors anywhere in the world.

The Canadian navy provides **assistance and support to other government departments** in many ways. One only has to think of its work with the Coast Guard, the RCMP, and the Department of Fisheries and Oceans to get some idea of the scope. But navies also support foreign policy, sending a variety of diplomatic messages in a way that armies and aircraft can never do because of their ships' unique legal status. Naval vessels are actually part of their country of origin just as embassies are. The mere presence of a warship, alone or as part of an international task force, can help to stabilize unrest through its deterrent effect (Adriatic in mid-90s); sometimes it can act as an ambassador, evacuating and sheltering nationals or adding support to an embassy in a trouble spot (Haiti in 1987-88); and at other times it can simply display its nation's concern over a developing situation (Jamaica in 1979).

Countries also use naval vessels diplomatically to "show the flag" which means they make visits to foreign nations to support trade missions and other international objectives. Lately, the Canadian government has shown a desire to increase our trade internationally and fully recognizes the navy's usefulness in this regard. On these goodwill visits it is, of course, the ships' crews who are the unofficial diplomats and who always bring a little bit of their home to the host nation. It is here where, hopefully, more understanding and respect between the peoples is initiated, in addition to the official objective of improving trade and diplomatic ties.

Fostering a voice with one's allies and having some influence in the quest for world peace is also part of a navy's diplomatic role. For example, Canadian ships participating in NATO's Standing Naval Force Atlantic have earned us respect of the other NATO members, especially since Canada's withdrawal of troops and aircraft from Germany. The navy 's involvement in NATO exercises and operations has become Canada's most visible presence in the western alliance and one we cannot do without. The new millennium also sees Canada actively expanding contacts and exchanges with the Asia-Pacific, Latin-American, and African regions These expressions of naval diplomacy are essential ways for a medium power to maintain influence in the world's deliberations and desire for peace.

Certain advocacy groups, such as the Naval Officers' Association of Canada, have a growing concern that some groups and individuals, including the present Liberal government, are over-emphasizing the navy's participation in overseas operations, which are expensive and at times can be highly dangerous. Moves in this direction can be traced to "vote getting" in most instances, because recent polls show that peacekeeping is an acceptable way to justify the CF and our navy. The Naval Officers' Association of Canada cautions us in the defence review of 1994:

"We think a different perspective on the maritime aspect is appropriate today. This perspective deals with the broader issue of ocean policy and the part maritime and naval forces play in this issue. Our thesis is that maritime defence or maritime security is only one segment of the larger context of our management and control of the ocean resources at our doorstep.

"Much of the discussion in the public arena has focused on the international side of defence policy and the roles of the military in the world. Peacekeeping has become a catchword. Indeed, some would have [our] entire armed forces devoted to becoming the military arm of the United Nations--in my view a very poor justification for a national military force.

...what are being overlooked are the major national maritime interests of this country. We have overlooked our national maritime security interests because the naval forces intended to provide support to NATO in the North Atlantic and to Canada-US regional pacts in the North Pacific by their very presence did the national function as a collateral task. The ships and aircraft of Maritime Command conducted long-range surveillance and exercised national presence in waters of vital interest to

this country on a daily basis. The fact that they were there in the first place because of Cold War factors does not change the equation.[36]

Other groups, like Canada 21*, see the issue quite differently and want Canada to have a constabulary (law enforcement) rather than a peacekeeping navy. They recommended the abolition of ASW and the Canadian Submarine Service. A direction such as this would prevent us using our naval forces in support of our foreign policy, either diplomatically or in multilateral efforts with any risk. This would be a step towards isolationism and Canada's withdrawal from the world's councils and affairs, an action few Canadians would support if push came to shove. A police-force navy would also involve some loss of sovereignty--being unable to respond to threatening incidents as part of an alliance degrades the respect a nation has around the world.

As far reaching as Maritime Command's roles are, they need to be evaluated at the dawn of the 21st century in the light of the new legislation regarding our oceans, because this has a major impact on understanding the need for a Canadian navy. Canada's new Oceans Act may not have added new roles to the navy, but it has significantly increased its tasks and responsibilities. The act came out of UNCLOS II but, when coupled with the Osbaldeston's 1990 study[37] on the utilization of the various Canadian fleets, the means of implementing our ocean management effectively became multi-agency, with the navy often in the lead role. The amalgamation of the Canadian Coast Guard and the DFO fleets under the Department of Fisheries and Oceans has been the most salient development since 1994 affecting our sovereignty. The broad requirements of Canada's Oceans Act has brought ships and aircraft of other government departments *into* naval task forces for specific operations, which are increasing annually. To give some idea of the increased scope: since 1990, ship days for fisheries patrols have grown by 300% and maritime air patrols are up by

---

*The Canada 21 Council prepared a document in response to the 1994 White Paper on Defence that was published by the Centre for International Studies at the University of Toronto. The council had representatives from the media, politics, academia and the armed forces.

700%. The navy responds to thousands of calls for search and rescue assistance, and saved sixty lives in 1991 alone. Maritime Air Group provided humanitarian aid to seventy others in the same period and is often responsible for collecting the evidence of pollution infractions by foreign shipping.

Since the 1994 White Paper, the navy has led the inter-departmental coordination of maritime enforcement plans. "Because naval units have modern communications and data processing equipment, they are ideally suited to coordinate the activities of units of other agencies in a common task."[38] Naval ships provide excellent on-the-spot command posts. Fifteen maritime sovereignty joint operations have been conducted on both coasts since 1994. MARCOT (an annual naval exercise on each coast) now includes Coast Guard, fisheries, and RCMP vessels and personnel. All the agencies share data through a communication system called CANMARNET, which is being further developed to handle the high volume of surveillance data that is projected. This will be fully integrated between all agencies. However, it is only the naval vessels that can provide the capabilities of large area surveillance, underwater surveillance, co-ordination and control, sustained operations, and, if necessary, firepower.

Whether the navy can actually achieve all that the Oceans Act requires is questionable. The replacement submarines will help but the navy needs new seaborne helicopters, upgrades for the *Aurora* maritime patrol aircraft, and the replacement of the three aging replenishment ships. We need all these to be a good steward of our seas and of our planet, by providing the ability to know what is happening in our vast waters and to intervene if necessary. Our government needs to get behind their new ocean strategy with meaningful actions in this direction.

Abroad, maritime peacekeeping operations have increased in frequency, complexity, and numbers since 1985, due to an unstable world order and partly because Canadian governments have learned that sending our forces overseas earns them votes and respect domestically and internationally. The Canadian navy participated in only four multilateral operations in the thirty-eight years from 1947 to 1985, but in four in the five years between 1985 and 1990. Since then our navy has been busier in far away places than at any time since the Korean War--employed in resolving crises in Europe, North America, the Caribbean, Africa and Southeast Asia, often in harm's way, in support of preserving peace. Our latest defence policy indicates that Canada will continue to deploy our navy abroad with the understanding that our involvement will not be unlimited. We have neither the numbers of vessels nor the capabilities required to do that and protect the sovereignty of our own seaward real estate.

Since the Cold War, the value of the Canadian navy has been amazing, given that it is so small. Some highlights of our navy's accomplishments are important to remember. Internationally our navy has:

- been part of the operation in East Timor;

- participated in liberating Kuwait with the UN coalition;

- enforced UN sanctions of Iraq after the Gulf War (and still does);

- coordinated the Canadian disaster relief in Florida after Hurricane Andrew;

- supported UN humanitarian relief in Somalia;

- re-established peace in Cambodia with UN forces;

- acted as observers in former Yugoslavia;

- enforced a UN embargo in the Adriatic sea; and,

- provided ships for interdiction operations off Haiti.

At home, the navy has:

- participated in joint and combined operations with other elements of our armed services and those of other countries in multilateral operations;

- provided 100 ship days/year to other government departments;

- provided 1000 aircraft days/year to other government departments;

- contributed to successful drug interdictions on both coasts. In 1985 off Nova Scotia, in 1987 off BC, in 1990 at Sydney, NS, in 1993 in Laredo Inlet, BC, in 1993 off Newfoundland, in 1994 off Shelburne NS, and again in 1998 off the BC coast;

- contributed to the operations surrounding the apprehension of ships carrying illegal immigrants off the BC coast in 1999;

- contributed to prevention of depletion of our fish stocks by foreign fleets;

- collected evidence of maritime pollution by foreign ships in our waters. (Our maritime patrol aircraft discover 85% of all maritime pollution.);

- prevented pollution of PEI when naval divers sealed a sunken oil barge; and,

- conducted 80% of all search and rescue operations.

Rarely has Maritime Command been so operationally active as it is now--since the Berlin Wall collapsed and the Cold War ended. With all this activity, every Canadian should have no difficulty in understanding why Canada needs a navy--a navy which has equipment that is modern, capable, and safe for the men and women that serve in it.

Chapter Seven
WHAT KIND OF NAVY?

Challenges abound as planners consider the ideal navy for Canada. The navies of medium powers with limited budgets are designed and developed around the traditional principle of sea control, taking into account the size and type of their ocean responsibilities, the use of their nation's waters, and their international obligations. In Canada's case, one naval expert summarized the resulting dilemma:

> "There is... a real challenge in developing a coherent fleet capability. On the one hand, nationally oriented defence requirements demand a fleet capable of comprehensive surveillance and local sea control, in which extensive warfighting capability is not essential. On the other hand, contributions to world order and stability require a navy with blue water, global reach, and the ability to counter and defeat adversaries equipped with the most sophisticated weapons. Naval requirements for each role are radically different and present their own challenges. The envisioned nationally oriented roles need more hulls but not necessarily more advanced technology. Collective

security commitments require high tech ships capable of operating in a high multi-threat environment which, by cost alone, tend to reduce overall fleet size.[39]

In the final analysis, Canada's political masters decide what type of navy we shall have because they approve or deny the funding. Then and only then can the navy implement the policy. However, the navy has the expertise to design the fleet and does so, recommending the size and make-up it must have to accomplish the responsibilities the government demands. Qualities that characterize maritime forces in support of government policies are readiness, self-sustainability, flexibility, and mobility. If the government of the day chooses to forgo or delay some of the navy's recommendations, it results in the navy abandoning some tasks or conducting their tasks less effectively, possibly placing personnel at risk. Spending cuts to an already poorly funded force, like Canada's, reduce readiness, sometimes to unacceptable levels.

Apart from finances, probably the major factor that has influenced the structure of navies, and will influence them into this new century, was the declaration of 200 nautical mile Exclusive Economic Zones following the UN Convention of the Law of the Sea. In Canada we followed this up with our Oceans Act, the implications of which increased the roles and responsibilities of our navy as well as its operational area.

Map 2 shows, in a way words can never do, the Canadian navy's areas of responsibility. It also shows how the three oceans are divided between the two commands, Atlantic and Pacific. Each with their own commander, Maritime Forces Atlantic (MARLANT), based in Halifax, NS, is responsible for the Atlantic areas and half the Arctic and Maritime Forces Pacific (MARPAC), based in Esquimalt, BC, looks after the Pacific and the other half of the Arctic, totaling 11,000,000 sq. km. Both areas include not only our sovereign territory, but also the areas assigned to us by our alliances. Both coasts draw information from a variety of military and civilian sources and other government departments to develop pictures of maritime activity taking place in our areas of responsibility. MARLANT can already produce a real-time surveillance picture that extends halfway across the north Atlantic--an area of 1.4 million sq. km.

The Canadian navy is unable to supply a full monitoring capability in our claimed territory as international law requires. Over the years prior to the mid-90s, our fleet diminished in size and capability due to neglect, while the responsibilities grew and developed with different emphases. Increasing challenges to our seaward sovereignty, more intergovernmental agency work, and the growth in the importance of the Asia-Pacific region widened the gap. The new frigates, the new Victoria class submarines, and the coastal defence vessels are a step in the right direction, but our shipborne helicopters and our replenishment vessels must be replaced. One other very important point that must be borne in mind in making force structure decisions is: while more sophisticated vessels can perform lesser tasks, the reverse is *never* true.

Canada has adopted a maritime strategy for the 21st century of using task groups at home or abroad, which can include submarines, with a coastal fleet made up of smaller vessels. The concept of operations is one of surveillance, patrol, presence, and response above, on, and below our seas.

As the Canadian navy's missions evolved from deep ocean ASW and convoy escort work to sovereignty protection and multilateral operations, the make-up of the fleet has changed too:

> *"National requirements call for a substantial surveillance capability and a high degree of responsiveness. The operating environment requires strong ships with good seakeeping capabilities and high endurance. International operations place greater stress on reach and sustainability but do not necessarily demand the capacity for power projection. Foreign operations demand the ability to operate successfully in a multi-threat environment, opposed by navies and air forces equipped with the most modern weapons systems."*[40]

A diverse and changing world order demands diverse defence. To react alone or with allies to meet threats to security interests comes at a cost that is mitigated by choosing small, modern, mobile, flexible, and diverse forces. If it must be small, it *must* be modern.

Flexibility, then, is the key characteristic our navy should have into 2020. Primarily, the fleet must be designed to meet Canada's national requirements, comprising 75% of its workload. But if the fleet structure is flexible enough it will also allow us to contribute overseas as part of an alliance at a meaningful, but not a high, intensity level.

"Multi-purpose" and "combat-capable" are two of the current watchwords that the Department of National Defence uses to describe the kind of navy that Canada needs to serve our current and future requirements. "Multi-purpose" means we recognize that threats at home and abroad are no longer predictable and the fleet needs to maintain some capability in most areas of naval warfare. Although Canada has de-emphasized anti-submarine warfare (ASW) and focused more on operations requiring the vessels to be more versatile, skilled ASW must remain a crucial capability for multilateral missions, as well as the foundation for domestic surveillance. "Combat-capable" recognizes that the navy is different from the Coast Guard or a fisheries protection services in certain core capabilities--specifically those necessary to fight and protect itself in conflicts. Someone (long forgotten) once said, "If it uses ammunition, it's core. If it doesn't, it ain't core." So core capabilities are understood to be those ships and skills without which the Canadian navy cannot function in a conflict--the "must haves," in other words. The navy considers submarines to be one of the "must haves."

Another adjective also heard describing a suitable navy for Canada is "balanced." Because our oceans do not just have a surface, but above-the-sea and under-the-sea components too, "balance" implies that we need, or may need, a presence in all three parts of the ocean's water column. Ships, shore-based and shipborne maritime aircraft, submarines, and fixed systems make up a "balanced" navy and each brings its own attributes to the equation. All are needed--to lose one of them reduces our navy's ability to do its mandated job significantly more than the loss suggests. For example, the range of our Halifax class frigates anti-surface capability would be reduced by a factor of three without aircraft-supplied data.

As our navy needs to be all these things and affordable too, some believe that a fully capable, balanced fleet of adequate size is out of reach. Another belief is the idea that if a crisis arose, we could expand the navy to the required level. Is this feasible? It is unlikely that sufficient time, even in protracted conflicts, would be available to upgrade or to build new warships--they take ten to fifteen years to get from concept to operational. In fact, it is more likely to be the new expertise that we cannot develop in time. So even if Canada was able to upgrade her navy fast enough to meet a sudden demand, the sailors' training might not catch up. This happens because not only do personnel have to be able to use the new equipment, they have to be able to integrate it with the fleet, the army and air force, and other countries' armed forces as well.

Where does Canada need to have a presence to effectively monitor our maritime territory, as international law tells us we must? This question has three parts: How many ships, submarines, and aircraft do we need? What capabilities must these units have? And where will they operate?

To do the job properly at home we need a lot--perhaps more than we can ever hope to afford, though having a submarine component makes this easier. So we have to try and provide coverage of our ocean areas with less. Also, sovereignty protection differs somewhat between the Atlantic and Pacific. In the east it mostly involves our commercial fisheries: on the head and tail of the Grand Banks, in Georgian Bay, and in the Davis Strait. On the west coast, sovereignty protection focuses more on supporting the UN ban on drift net fishing beyond our EEZ, combating drug and migrant smugglers who consider the coves and inlets of BC some of the safest places in the world to unload people and narcotics, and in defusing the Salmon Wars with the Alaskan fishery. Excluding the high Arctic, which can only be patrolled by air at present, there are seven crucial ocean areas where Canada should have the ability to perform surveillance patrols and be able to respond to incursions that might affect our sovereignty. They are:

- the Georges Bank and the approaches to the Bay of Fundy;

- the approaches to Halifax and the Scotia Shelf;

- the approaches to the Cabot Strait and the Gulf of St Lawrence;

- the Grand Banks, including the Nose and Tail;

- the Strait of Belle Isle, the southern Labrador Sea, the Davis Strait, Baffin Bay and the choke points of the Arctic Archipelago;

- the ocean approaches to the Strait of Juan de Fuca; and

- the ocean approaches to the northern British Columbia waters: Queen Charlotte Sound, Dixon Entrance and the Gulf of Alaska. (The two Pacific areas cover 383,690 sq. kms.)

We can determine the types and numbers of naval assets needed to monitor these areas by looking at the individual capabilities of ships, submarines, and aircraft. Modern submarines can detect surface and underwater contacts over about 125,000 square kilometers and can maintain this coverage for 40-50 days without support. Sometimes the submarine can establish the probable identity from its acoustic signature, but more often has to get close to contacts to identify them through the periscope. This is time-consuming and it is much more efficient to get a long range maritime patrol aircraft to do it if the contact is on the surface. On a ten-hour patrol an *Aurora* can cover about 300,000 square kilometers, but it is limited in its response to any hostile contact it might find. One of Canada's new frigates can only survey 32,000 square kilometers for eight to ten days without support, but can track, identify, and respond to contacts above, on, and below the ocean. A modern seaborne helicopter used in conjunction with a frigate can increase this area for limited periods and has the advantage of being able to identify the contact, as well as put boarding parties onto surface ships if necessary.

However, a combination of surface and air forces can cover a slightly bigger area than just one submarine, though at much greater cost. For example, four frigates with helicopters and a replenishment ship can cover about 192,000 square kilometers (equivalent to all the Great Lakes) for thirty days. Add a submarine to the task group of five ships and aircraft and you have an even more effective, flexible combination. But if you delete one of the three components, the effectiveness drops, and drops out of all proportion to the loss. A former submarine squadron commander[41] once said, "If you have to make do with only one of the three components, keep the submarines; if you can only afford two, keep the submarines and aircraft." That one submarine can be acquired and operated at one third of the cost of one frigate, makes them even more attractive to a fiscally restrained sovereign nation. The issue then, is not choosing between aircraft, submarines, or frigates because they provide different capabilities. It is their synergy as a team that is so dramatic--together they are much more than a sum of their parts.

Fixed underwater systems can provide a good deal of the surveillance part of the sea control package for relatively lower cost, especially if placed across entrances and exits of certain transit routes. However, arrays like this can only tell the navy that a vessel is passing or in the vicinity. A credible response requires dispatching an appropriate platform--an aircraft, ship(s), a submarine, or a combination of the three.

If Canada wants a task group in all the seven strategic areas off Canada's coasts, the math is simple. The Canadian navy would be made up of seven submarines, twenty-one frigates, seven upgraded destroyers, fifty-six helicopters and seven replenishment ships on station, plus more in maintenance routines. Say it takes four maritime patrol aircraft to maintain continuous patrol in each area, we should also have thirty-five *Aurora's* in the air and several more back-ups on the ground. Even with all these, all our fishing grounds would not be covered.

In the early 1990s, the navy adopted the task group concept as its strategic centrepiece. This flexible organization can comprise any fleet units required to accomplish a specific mission, but is limited by the *1994 Defence White Paper* to no more than four major combatants (destroyers, frigates, or submarines) and one replenishment ship. Task groups are able to provide sea control, either independently or with fleet units of other navies.

VESSEL(S)	COVERAGE	ENDURANCE	COST/DAY
4 surface ships + 1 replenishment ship	192,000 sq. km	30 days	About $2 million
1 patrol frigate with shipborne helicopter	69,000 sq. km	10 days	$148,000.00
1 maritime patrol aircraft	300,000 sq. km	10 hours	$151,000.00
1 diesel/electric submarine	125,000 sq. km	50 days	Os - $59,000.00 Vics - $20,000.00

Table 2: Comparison of coverage, endurance and cost of a variety of Canadian naval surveillance platforms.

Using this task group structure, the Conference of Defence Associations (CDA) recommended in 1994 the following fleet for the new millennium[42] five maritime task groups (each with three frigates, one modernized destroyer, one replenishment ship and up to eight helicopters), six submarines, five squadrons of maritime patrol aircraft, and a coastal surveillance and defence organization, all maintained under a three-tier readiness system. The conference described the infrastructure to support this navy as including one naval base with dockyards and one maritime air base on each coast, which we already have. CDA stated that submarines and aircraft should augment the task group formations to provide better surveillance over our very large ocean areas and to maintain the fleet's ASW proficiency. However, they also clarified, short of all-out war, Canada's seven areas do not need to be patrolled all the time. Experience shows that effective surveillance and presence can be accomplished with less because intruders can never be certain where the task force or sub/air team will be deployed.

However, the present Canadian fleet cannot meet all the CDA's concept of operations. We are short of the required number of vessels, even with the new Victorias coming on stream. We would have to add frigates, replenishment ships (three to replace the present aging AORs and two new), two more submarines than we are getting, fixed acoustic surveillance systems for the Arctic and coastal waters, one additional maritime patrol aircraft squadron, and forty new shipborne helicopters. Is this realistic? Probably not--although the full package still amounts to only $5.00/square kilometre of ocean for which we are responsible. So we must prioritize--the submarines, shipborne helicopters, and new replenishment ships are the top three requirements. One down, two to go.

Canada's present inventory looks like this. The navy has twelve new Halifax class frigates. The four older Tribal class destroyers have been well modernized for air defence, as well as for command and control. Twelve maritime coastal defence vessels are built or under construction, which will be manned mostly by reservists and will provide a mine countermeasure capability. One replenishment ship (of the three), HMCS *Provider*, which was to be paid off, has been kept in service because of the increasing need to sealift personnel, equipment and supplies for multilateral operations. Once mostly on the Atlantic coast, the navy's ships are now more evenly distributed between the Pacific and Atlantic coasts, in recognition of the growing importance of the Asia-Pacific region. Maritime Air Group has the thirty aging Sea King helicopters, eighteen *Aurora* and three *Arcturus* long-range patrol aircraft, and other support aircraft for the navy's operations based on both coasts. In 1994, HMCS *Trinity*, an integrated surveillance system centre, opened in Halifax. *Trinity* is part of a global network of fixed and mobile acoustic sensors whose data is shared amongst western allies.

At the end of the 1990s, faced with an increasing number of operations, expensive procurement needs, and tight fiscal parameters, the navy developed a structure based on the task group concept coupled with tiered readiness. No longer can Maritime Command afford to keep all its ships at a uniform level of readiness as it has in the past. At the start of the new millennium, Canada has enough ships to have one task group on each coast: made up of one destroyer, two frigates, one submarine (when the Victorias arrive), one replenishment ship, and up to seven helicopters and six maritime patrol aircraft each. One is designated the Contingency Task Group, earmarked for deployment within thirty days to trouble spots, and one as the National Task Group, which is on sixty day readiness. Ships used for the Standing Naval Force Atlantic or carrier battle group operations will be taken from these two task groups. The rest of the fleet is now kept at a lower level of operational readiness than before.

The navy has designated their new readiness levels as high, standard, and extended. High means that the vessels are fully worked up, certified in all weapons systems, and maintained at a level of technical readiness that permits deployment to an area of mid-intensity operations within twenty-one days. To maintain this proficiency, ships in this tier will require 120 days/year at sea. Also, there is one ship on each coast designated as the ready duty ship, able to deploy in hours--not days. Ships in the standard tier will be able to perform routine sovereignty operations, participate in national and international exercises, and conduct personnel training. These ships need about eighty-sea days/year. They could, if required, deploy to a mid-intensity conflict within ninety days. The extended tier ships are the harbour training vessels and those in refit or work periods. They will be at sea for very limited periods (less than twenty days/year) and would take 180 days to be ready for deployment

Then we come to our sub-surface component--also considered a "core capability." Up to 2000, we had one over-age Oberon class submarine (two had already been paid-off to save money), based on the Atlantic coast. Once all the Victoria class boats join the fleet, three will operate from the east coast and one from the west. As one of the most cost-effective warships and the only vessel capable of important underwater surveillance, submarines do provide the "balance" for the Canadian fleet. Maritime Command has made the integration of the Victoria submarines into the task groups its top operational priority for the next few years. Three of the new submarines will be kept at high readiness while one will always be in the extended category.

And last, but certainly not least, are the 8,930 very professional personnel who allow the navy to achieve its capability, as long as they are kept highly trained. Morale is reported to be high in the Canadian navy, largely because the fleet has been so busy in the last decade and because of the arrival of new ships and submarines. Much of the activity has been in multilateral operations and those involved feel that they are making a significant contribution to the national interest of Canada and the world.

Broad-based capabilities and efficiency are the key components of the vessels Canada requires to manage our huge maritime areas. The capabilities have to be "mission related" and so our ships need to be designed to provide excellent monitoring abilities in three oceans, sufficiently safe to be sent in harm's way on multilateral operations of medium intensity, and have good sea-keeping characteristics. To opponents of this concept of operations and structure who advocate for a police force navy of smaller vessels, the experts say small ships may cost less but come with a proportionate loss of capability--a loss we cannot live with given our defence policy. Sophisticated ships can effectively perform lesser tasks, but smaller ships cannot perform more complicated ones.

Surveillance and presence in the Arctic are a challenge to naval planners, for Canada has no nuclear-powered submarines and no icebreaker capable of year round passage through the Arctic straits. At present, our navy schedules one patrol a month by a maritime patrol aircraft. However, aircraft are limited in detection of and response to sub-ice vessels; fixed systems can monitor underwater, but cannot respond; submarines can monitor below the ice if they are equipped with some type of air independent power (AIP), but they do not have the ability to provide a graduated response. We need a varied approach to the Arctic challenge. The Atlantic and Pacific, in contrast, are more accessible than the Arctic and are easier to monitor with surface and sub-surface vessels but both have demanding acoustic properties on our continental shelf and very unpredictable weather. All of this adds up to the Canadian navy needing ships and submarines that have a high degree of flexibility and sea-worthiness, as well as long legs, for domestic security.

Moreover, however unpleasant submarine, missile, and aircraft threats are, our naval vessels face them when abroad on multilateral missions. For example, they were the reality when Canadian naval units were in the Adriatic and Persian Gulf. Our surface ships have to be able to counter anti-ship missiles, like the dreaded EXOCETs, as well as heavy-duty torpedoes from diesel/electric or nuclear-powered submarines. Inshore operations bring threats from fixed wing aircraft, shore-based missiles, helicopters, and mines--those easily deployed weapons that are able to produce a maritime threat out of all proportion to their cost. So air defence, anti-submarine warfare, and mine countermeasures are vital skills for our navy and they require expensive equipment and significant amounts of personnel training to develop and maintain.

Our modern navy has to be kept up-to-date to ensure the safety of our sailors, integrate well with our allies, and face opponents equipped with modern systems. This is a constant battle for naval planners at the turn of the century with the staggering acceleration of technology. The advances in data processing, artificial intelligence, database management, communications, sensors and weaponry, need vessels with reduced acoustic signatures, new stealth technologies, fuel cells to reduce noise and infrared signatures, and active noise cancellation. These, in their turn, will generate development of more sophisticated detection systems--a never-ending upward spiral.

Another vital component of our navy is its personnel; indeed, they are the key to efficiency and effectiveness. For unless the crews are skilled, the most up-to-date and expensive equipment will not perform to its potential. The cost of training (substitute "personal readiness" if you wish) is enormously expensive and must be factored into the type of navy we have. Less money in the budget could mean less training, which could have a serious impact on the effectiveness of the fleet, especially on medium intensity operations.

The skills of Canadian crews must not only be kept at a high standard, but also must be responsive to change as technology advances. Excellent training is just as vital as procuring the latest equipment. Canadian crews must maintain all the basic operational skills all the time, for it would be highly dangerous for them not to. These vital skills include: defensive anti-submarine warfare (ASW), missile defence and anti-air warfare (AAW), and anti-surface warfare (ASUW). A recent survey of areas needing the most improvement in the Canadian navy showed that ASW topped the list, and submarines are essential for this training. Other tasks for which the fleet must continuously train are: search and rescue; the provision of humanitarian assistance at sea and in coastal communities at home and abroad; the assistance of other government departments in areas such as fishery patrols, law enforcement, customs operations, and environmental control; mine warfare and explosive disposal; and the protection of shipping and coastal areas against military threats or maritime terrorism.

Moreover, the increased focus on coastal waters, domestically and internationally, presents additional training challenges for all western navies. With the reduction of the Soviet threat, much work in the open ocean has ceased--the West rules! The early part of the 2000s will see navies working in the shallow, littoral waters of their own countries and those of others when part of multilateral operations.

This switch from the deep ocean environment to shallow water demands that navies deal with very different sound characteristics, high traffic densities, and high ambient noise. Sanction enforcement, interdiction operations, support to amphibious and ground forces ashore, and contingency missions, all tend to demonstrate this current shift from the open ocean to coastal seas.

The characteristics of sound propagation in the coastal areas are quite different and more difficult than in the mid-ocean areas. Today the challenges in underwater operations lie in the detection and monitoring of activity on continental shelves. This relatively shallow water--less than 200 meters--is affected by all kinds of factors. There are layers of different temperatures and salinities in the sea that cause severe degradation of sound signals (sonar) in the water and mean that detection ranges are much less than in the open ocean. The warming of the surface in the summer, the effects of winds on the surface, and the mixing of warm and cold ocean currents effectively mask anything under 20 meters from surface detection. Close to shore, and in the shallow water of the continental shelf, the ambient noise is greater than in the deep ocean--the sounds of shipping concentrating near ports, fish, and shellfish drown out the noise generated by vessels that navies want to hear. In contrast, sound propagation in the Arctic Ocean is good. The Canadian Arctic waters have very little continental shelf, get deep rapidly, their ice cover prevents the mixing of layers and surface warming, and there is less ambient noise.

The ideal navy to uphold the government's defence policy is probably unreachable, unless future governments decide to allocate significantly more funding to the Department of National Defence. However, there has been major improvement in the past decade-- our navy has achieved an unprecedented level of operational capability, as well as interoperability with the USN, which allows Canada the flexibility to rapidly deploy ships on operations anywhere in the world. And we can be sure that our navy will continue to press for what it needs to do the job well and safely.

Chapter Eight
SUBMARINES ARE SPECIAL

"We come unseen"

Despite the contribution that Allied submarines made to winning WWII in Europe and the Pacific, most civilians in the post-war period perceived submarines to be sinister, ugly, claustrophobic, and having an unfair advantage. Perpetuated by the press and restricted by security considerations, the citizens' opinions were based on U-boats which were distinctly nasty if you were one of the Allies and awesomely capable if you were on the Axis side. In the forties, these submarines sank ships transporting desperately needed food and war supplies to a beleaguered Britain; submarines sank Canadian warships and merchant ships in the Atlantic, killing Canadian sailors; and submarines nearly sank the war for the Allies.

Today, when asked to describe submarines, the man-in-the-street uses adjectives like expensive, dangerous, lethal, and claustrophobic. He thinks mostly of nuclear-powered boats, not discriminating between those that carry nuclear missiles and those that don't. Submarines are inherently frightening to the average Joe and Jane. As one eminent Canadian submariner observed in 1991: "There seems to be a school of thought which believes that the major navies are engaging in dangerous, provocative, cat and mouse games beneath the seas (especially in the Arctic), and that such activities could lead to hostilities. ...such believers have been victims of 'Tom Clancy-ism'."[43] The average Canadian rarely mentions conventionally powered diesel-electric submarines, although they are in the vast majority. If asked what submarines do, he will still reply confidently, "Sink ships." Perceptions don't change all that much.

Canadian submariners, on the other hand, would use words like quiet, independent, and very effective. A listener would sense, rather than hear, the strong belief and pride behind their words.

Versatile is another adjective with which to describe modern submarines--whether they are diesel/electric, nuclear-powered, or use another form of air-independent power. They seem to be able to do most things but fly. They can operate under the ice, in deep ocean areas, and in restricted coastal waters; they can be used for myriad operations.

Submarines have many unique attributes that set them apart from other warships. It may be a little obvious to state, but no other vessel can operate underwater. The three dimensional nature of the maritime environment means that no single system can provide a capability in all dimensions and it is the underwater capability that makes the submarines so special.

Stealth, stemming from its diving capability, is the submarine's greatest characteristic. It is the trait that makes submarines stand alone amongst all other naval vessels, big and small; that makes submarines unique and versatile; and that gives submarines the advantage of surprise. Submarines can deploy in complete secrecy, can appear unexpectedly, and can or cannot be present, thus causing significant concern to any potential adversary or lawbreaker. They make their living underwater, hidden from most observers: "What you can't see, you can't hit!"[44] The submarine was the original stealth platform and has yet to be surpassed, despite millions of dollars being spent on stealth technology over the past few years. Naval experts talk about submarines being "covert," a word filled with negative connotations. They use the word to mean hidden, secret, concealed, or at least, being very hard to find--and it is this covertness that makes them so good at monitoring maritime activity on or below the surface, gathering intelligence, surprising illegal activity, and training the surface fleet in ASW. When a submarine deployed in complete secrecy suddenly reappears, it uses its gift of surprise and catches its adversary unprepared. Extend the elements of surprise and stealth a notch and you gain a characteristic called uncertainty. Just because you cannot see a submarine, you cannot be sure if it is not there. It might be or it might not--who's going to take the chance? A boat's possible presence can deter battle fleets from venturing onto the high seas or snakeheads from depositing some illegal immigrants.

Submarine endurance--another characteristic that sets submarines, even conventional ones, apart--is better than many surface ships. Their high fuel economy is a well-documented fact whether on the surface or submerged and whether they use standard marine fuels or nuclear power. Conventionally powered submarines can travel up to 15,500 nautical miles without refueling, using their diesel engines, thus roaming widely. At slow speeds standard batteries can last up to four days and improved batteries even longer, some up to twelve. Air independent power (AIP) can provide about fourteen to twenty days endurance and the prediction is that some systems will operate up to thirty days by 2005. Of course, nuclear-powered submarines do not need refueling in the conventional sense and are only limited by the endurance of their crews and the amount of supplies they can carry. If the men could take it, they could be on patrol indefinitely.

Another important attribute which is often forgotten, is the submarine's independence from the effects of the weather. Time after time in major maritime exercises, adverse weather calls a halt to activities on the surface and in the air, while submarines remain submerged and go about their business as usual. For Canada, this virtue is very important considering the harsh conditions that prevail in our northern waters.

When stealth, endurance, and surprise are combined, the submarine is clearly the least vulnerable, and therefore the most survivable, of all naval vessels. It is the only vessel that can operate underwater and the only vessel that can operate in areas where the air or shore threat is extreme. This is especially valuable off hostile coasts, where shore-based missiles and enemy aircraft can easily reach vessels needing to operate inshore, as happened recently in the Adriatic. Only the submarine can safely provide discreet surveillance, can insert small teams of commandos, and can deal with opposing submarines in coastal waters when the opponent has air superiority. They are most difficult to detect, attack, and neutralize. This ability to be relatively safe is one of the submarine's greatest assets and is essential to any navy serious about participating in peacekeeping.

Part of submarines' stealth capabilities also comes from how quietly they operate. As submarines can be heard underwater with passive sonar, the amount of noise they generate is critical to their remaining undetected. It is also critical to the amount they can hear--a noisy boat cannot detect surface or underwater contacts. Speed produces detectable noise, so the slower a boat goes, the quieter it is. The advantage goes to the boat that moves the least. Submarine designers and submariners are fixated about noise--theirs, first and foremost--and will do almost anything to avoid making any. Modern submarines are very, very quiet indeed, and added to that, their ability to dive below "the layer" makes them superb surveillance platforms.

Submarines also carry enormous punch. They can be equipped with a variety of torpedoes, missiles, and mines. In addition, though often overlooked, are the small teams of commandos submarines can insert into enemy territory for sabotage and intelligence purposes.

Independence is another valuable and defining characteristic of submarines. They alone, of all naval vessels, operate entirely independently, often out of contact with their operational command for weeks. They are mightily self-sufficient, not needing fuel or supplies every few days from a replenishment ship--like frigates and destroyers--and this simple fact adds to their stealth quotient.

Submarines carry small crews these days. Reduced complements open the prospect of double crewing a boat, which gives its owner two boats for the price of one. Double crewing a frigate would take about 450 personnel (including the air

DEEPLY CANADIAN 99

detachment), but only ninety plus for a submarine like the new Victorias.

Although specifications vary, modern boats can dive to depths of between 800 and 1500 feet, easily making them invisible from the air and surface for the foreseeable future. Normal operating depths are around 600-800 feet. Some Russian boats are reported to reach depths of more than 3000 feet but they do not operate routinely that far down due to the wear and tear on the hulls from such massive pressure changes.

High speed is not only the preserve of nuclear-powered boats nowadays, although sustained high speed is. Some diesel/electric boats can sprint at over 20 knots for ten to fifteen minutes, others for an hour or more, before their batteries are depleted and the submarine has to come close to the surface to snorkel for air to replenish them. Submarines use speed sparingly, as with speed comes noise--noise that others can hear and noise that deafens the submarine itself. Experts agree that boats cannot listen effectively at speeds over 25 knots. Diesel/electric submarines also use speed sparingly, because when running on their batteries, speeds around 20 knots deplete the stored power very quickly. This type of boat uses short high-speed sprints to get out of trouble fast or to zero in on a target quickly. However, they cannot use 20+ knots for long passages that might be required to relocate to a spot 1000 miles away. Navies that have vast operating areas or interests that are far from home benefit from submarines that get places fast but all, once they have arrived on station, stop roaring around at full power because someone will hear them. The limitations that batteries and lack of sustained speed imposes on diesel/electric boats are obvious. Firstly, they cannot hope to reach contacts their modern long-range passive sonar can detect far away. Secondly, in conflicts the need to come up for air can be very confining. At normal operating speeds, modern diesel/electric submarines do 12 knots on the surface and about 10 knots while snorkeling. If using the battery carefully, modern boats can travel underwater at 3-4 knots for over three days.

If not nuclear-powered, modern submarines have fuel capacities that provide ranges from 8000 to 15,500 nautical miles. Equally as important as diesel fuel, conventional boats can carry enough food, weapons, and other supplies to support patrols of up fifty days, and in times of desperate need, could probably manage at sea for up to ninety days without support of any kind. Of course, nuclear-powered boats can perform until the food runs out or the crew yells for mercy.

Submarines have become more manoeverable since the first use of the teardrop-shaped hull in the American Albacore/Skipjack design. The ability to reach a distant target, and more importantly, the ability to get away if detected by an opponent, is an essential requirement for a submarine. Submarines evade detection, torpedoes, and depth charges by varying their speed, depth, and location, sometimes slowly and stealthily, sometimes with violent evasive manoeuvres. Unlike surface vessels, submarine manoeuvrability has to be three-dimensional and is dependent on the boat's size, length and shape, power (underwater speed), and the depth to which it can dive. These factors vary between SSNs, SSKs, and SSBNs, as well as between classes. Generalizing somewhat and refraining from a heavy duty engineering approach, smaller submarines are more agile; larger boats have bigger, slower turning circles; and longer ones dive faster. However, it is safe to say that all submariners prefer to have a highly manoeuvrable boat in a squeeze.

The teardrop hull, short and fat at the bow and tapering at the stern, is more dynamically stable than the longer, slimmer variety typical of the WWII era. These older boats were designed for high surface speed and needed the narrow, long shape to reduce drag produced by the hull and waves. The classic teardrop shape is better suited to underwater operations, reducing drag below the surface by an amazing 40% and allowing hulls to be shorter and more manoeuvrable. Other advantages of the design include the space to have two or three decks below for more equipment and better habitability, and the need for less power to drive the submarine. Nowadays the teardrop shape has been modified--it is longer with a parallel mid-section, which serves to increase the internal volume of the boat.

Modern combat systems combine sensor, fire control (the torpedo firing system), data management, and navigation, and these reduce the workload of the operators. They feature multi-function consoles, standardized data buses, and modular design. Integrated combat systems provide invaluable assistance to the team throughout mission planning, detection, tracking, identification, and weapons launch.

"Noise," in submariners' terms, also includes non-acoustic ways of being detected, such as the infrared and electromagnetic wavelengths emitted by submarines. All are being successfully reduced these days. Modern boats are now very quiet--even the nuclear-powered variety that used to have a reputation of sounding like a truck thundering along underwater. Although quietening technologies have made substantial advances, diesel/electric boats are still considered quieter than nuclear-powered submarines. Noise arises from propeller cavitations, internal machinery, and the crew. Occasional sounds, usually brief, also occur when torpedo tube doors are opened, torpedoes are fired, or when violent evasive manoeuvres have to be executed. Modern techniques employed to reduce emitted sound from current submarines include: methods to reduce machinery vibration and its transmission to the hull; more hydrodynamic hull shapes; double-hull construction; sound absorbing materials; better propeller design; and innovative propulsion systems. Submarine stealth is an industry all by itself. Today outer hulls are coated with anechoic tiles, which absorb active sonar rather than return it; machinery is mounted on rubber or pneumatic sound mounts to reduce noise that could be detected by passive sonar; isolation techniques put machinery on "floating" rafts so that vibration cannot be transmitted to the hull; active vibration suppression cancels noise by introducing a sound signal equal in amplitude but opposite in phase to the offending frequency; and advanced propeller designs use low r.p.ms and skewed blades to reduce cavitation sounds. New pump jets can get rid of the need for propellers altogether.

Detection techniques have kept pace with noise reduction-- the quieter the boats have become, the more sensitive the sensors to find them need to be. Modern submarines are equipped with surveillance systems which are their eyes and ears. The most obvious are the search and attack periscopes--the true eyes of the boat. They can be used above the waves and, surprisingly to most landlubbers, down to 120 feet to look closely at ships' hulls, propellers, etc. A submarine's radar, also on a raisable mast like the periscope, is mostly used for navigation because it is an active sensor, emitting signals that can be detected by others intent on finding the submarine. When on the surface or at periscope depth the electronic surveillance measures (ESM) system is used to detect radar or communications transmissions from others at great distances. This system, on a mast, also enables the submarine to classify the contact--is it a fishing boat, a warship, or a cruise ship? But most importantly, ESM gives early warning of threats from the air, like helicopters. Other submarine sensors, which always can be retrofitted, include: state-of-the-art torpedo warning sonar; mine-detection sonar; underwater communications; echo sounders; and upward-looking sonar and TV for operating under ice.

Sonar is the sensor most individuals think of when asked to describe how submarines detect activity around them. Active sonar, the one that pings, is the best known, having been widely dramatized in movies. But it is the passive systems that are the real "eyes" of the boat, though "long ears" would be a more accurate description, and these provide the modern submarine with its extraordinary monitoring capability and accuracy when attacking targets.

Passive or listening sonar did not begin to gain sophistication until after WWII, when the advent of the snorkel kept the submarine below the surface much more. Before then, submarines were vessels that detected and attacked targets on the surface using the human eye and resorted to diving only to evade pursuers. It was the lack of lookouts when snorkeling that forced the development of a technology to replace them. Early passive sonar provided only the bearing of contacts (where they were in relation to the listener) but later calculating range (distance) became possible and accurate enough to enable the systems to be linked to the boat's torpedo firing system, known as the fire control system. Later still came the ability to classify contacts. This is the capability to pinpoint what type of vessel it might be--a surface ship or submarine--perhaps even as accurately as a destroyer or carrier. But identification of which vessel it is *by name* is usually done visually. The further the contact is from the listener, the more difficult it becomes to do an accurate target motion analysis (TMA) and classification. Even so the advances in passive sonar have been amazing--modern submarines can detect, track, and classify several sound sources at the same time, often at great distances.

The challenge remaining for submariners is the changing acoustic characteristics of the ocean, especially in shallow waters--one day is always different from the next. Salinity, temperature, bottom characteristics, and depth of the ocean all change the speed and paths of sound waves. Muddy seabeds absorb sound; rocks increase the background clutter and large ones can mimic realistic submarine contacts; the marginal ice zones (the Gulf of St. Lawrence is one) produce pack ice, icebergs, shallow fresh water, and fog; and tidal currents add to the complexity. Operators need to know the characteristics of the acoustic environment in which they are working and many potential operating areas for multilateral forces have never been investigated. The computer has made the art of passive sonar easier for the operators, though most would contend that sound waves still seem to have minds of their own and all acknowledge that a skillfully operated diesel/electric boat can be well nigh impossible to find in certain circumstances.

Modern passive sonar includes hull-mounted systems and towed arrays. There are two main sensors on the hull--usually a series of low frequency flank arrays and a bow mounted sonar--and while they both detect low frequency sound, they do slightly different jobs. The flank arrays consist of many ranging transducers placed the length of both sides of the boat and provide the control room with the bearing and range of multiple contacts out beyond 200 miles if the acoustic conditions are good, less if not. The large wrap-around bow sonars are used to pinpoint contacts more accurately when they are closer, within about 30 miles, and provide very accurate bearings and ranges for weapons firing solutions. Both sonars are linked to the fire control system and detect the noise that all contacts emit from machinery and propellers, etc., which are so distinctive for individual vessels. Sonar operators are able to classify contacts from their sound signatures, either exactly by comparison with a library of stored signatures or more generically.

Towed surveillance arrays (TAS), which are not always installed, are streamed astern of some submarines and also capture the low frequency emissions. The advantage of a towed sonar system is that it gets the listening device away from the noise of the towing submarine, greatly improving reception. Towed arrays can detect contacts at 200 miles but it can take hours for a crew to develop a meaningful target motion analysis if the data is fragmented or intermittent, as it often is from so far away. Any submarine hoping to intercept such a contact needs sustained high speed to travel the distance to reach it and diesel/electric boats often have to delegate the interception to another member of the ASW team.

As submarines have got quieter and submariners have become more skilled at hiding in the layers of the sea, there comes a time when the ASW team has to resort to active sonar--the pinging variety--to locate their adversary. The following example shows just how hard this really is to do: during an exercise in 1995, a seven ship task group filled the shallow English Channel with active sonar trying to find a Dutch submarine they knew was there. They never detected it hiding by a wreck, and later the boat "torpedoed" five of the surface ships.

Active sonar systems send out a pulse of sound that bounces off a contact and returns. The time delay of this returning echo provides accurate range of a contact as long as there is no bending of the rays. So, used as a last resort and very sparingly, active sonar can be accurate in localizing the target when it is close and provides good data for fire control. All modern submarines carry at least one active system, often in the bow, that sends out pings in frequencies from 10-30 kHz. Depending on the frequency used and the water conditions, active sonar can reach out, discover, and determine ranges of contacts over a relatively short distance. We are not there yet, but American experts are predicting that it *may* be possible to disguise the revealing ping as another sound found in the ambient noise of the sea--a burping whale for instance--which would preserve the invisibility of the transmitting vessel.

Submarine sensors today are many and sophisticated. They require huge amounts of electrical power to operate, massive data processing capability, and very highly trained sailors to operate them successfully. "The early part of the time on patrol would be spent in learning the area: its hydrographic, environmental and acoustic conditions, traffic patterns, etc. Getting to know the 'personality' of one's area is a classic submarine practice."[45]

Weapons are the equipment that make ships and submarines "combat-capable" or, in other words, able to fight. Without them, they would be a coastguard or merchant submarine. Modern diesel/electric submarines can deliver as devastating a blow as any nuclear-powered submarine because they carry the same weapons. Typically they carry heavyweight torpedoes like the American Mark 48 ADCAP (short for Advanced Capability) or the British *Spearfish* that are dual purpose weapons suitable for use against surface ships or submarines, anti-surface missiles, like the Sub-Harpoon, and mines.

Capable of travelling at about 70 knots, guided by the submarine that launched it, and getting quieter every year, the modern heavyweight torpedo is one of the most lethal weapons in the naval inventory today, sinking ships by exploding below the hull and breaking the vessel's back. They are also one of the most expensive weapons--the Mark 48 ADCAP used in Canadian submarines costs over $1 million a pop.

Mines, manufactured in over twenty countries in the thousands, are an extraordinarily effective means of sea control-- they are cheap, easily laid, and have a powerful deterrent effect on an opponent. Experts consider the modern mine is more dangerous to submarines than any other ASW weapon and history reminds us that fully one third of the submarines lost in WWII were lost to mines. Mines are part of the submarine arsenal too--boats can lay mines from the same tubes as torpedoes in shallow or deep waters and even under ice where no surface minelayer can go, giving versatility to any navy that may wish to deny access to shipping lanes and ports.

Submarines can also launch land attack missiles, anti-ship cruise missiles, and ICBMs. France, China, Russia and the US make these types of weapons, and some require special launchers. Neither missiles nor mines have ever been carried by Canadian submarines nor will they be in 2000 onward.

Traditional tactical roles of submarines are giving way to a new set of roles. These new roles will not replace the old ones, but will augment them, and are likely to be emphasized more in the coming century. Peter Haydon, a prominent Canadian naval writer, lists the following roles for the world's submarines as we enter the new millennium:

• Underwater scientific research and surveys;

- A wide range of training services;

- Surveillance, monitoring, and verification operations (in ocean approaches and for advance warning);

- Intelligence gathering--learning about the operations of foreign vessels;

- Reconnaissance of harbours, coastlines, and shore defences for peacekeeping purposes;

- Blockading ports and waterways and denying an adversary use of bodies of water (can use force to ensure compliance);

- Special operations (always covert);

- Attacking shipping and other submarines;

- Attacking shore targets;

- Minelaying; and

- Launching strategic weapons (deterrence).

The traditional role most Canadians identify submarines with is sinking ships. This will continue in medium and high intensity conflicts around the world, as will sinking other submarines. However, Canadian submarines have never done much "sinking of ships." *CC1* and *CC2* in WWI started out undertaking that role but the targets never materialized and it is doubtful if the crews were well trained enough at the beginning of the war to accomplish it. We did not have our own submarines in WWII with which to sink ships, but most of the twenty-six Canadian submariners serving in British boats were involved in it. Because of their ship-sinking ability, submarines have played a key role in modern versions of the medieval siege--where armies of knights starved a castle into submission, submarines can now starve a whole country into capitulation. Submarine siege warfare, very nearly successful in WWII when the U-boats decimated the convoys supplying Britain, has not been a part of the Canadian submarine squadron's experience, though it is part of their repertoire. However today's sieges are more likely to be embargoes and blockades in regional conflicts, as were conducted in the Gulf War and the Adriatic.

Intelligence gathering, reconnaissance, and other covert activities, which utilize the submarine's stealth, have always been primary roles for the world's submarine services. These activities came into their own during WWII and many Canadians were exposed to them in Canadian, European, and Far Eastern waters. They rescued French Resistance workers fleeing from the Gestapo and allied saboteurs in the Far East. They inserted teams of commandos and carried chariots and their crews to enemy ports in the Mediterranean and the Far East. Submarines gathered information for the Sicilian landings and the raids on the German battleship, *Tirpitz*. In the Cold War, the Canadian Oberon class submarines did their share of shadowing Soviet boats, practising their skills of submarine versus submarine. Recently submarines conducted reconnaissance in the Adriatic of ship, troop and equipment movements, and the shore installations in the former Yugoslavia. Most importantly, they also were able to provide early warning of Serbian submarine activity off the coast of Bosnia.

Submarines can also be used against states that attempt to interrupt or threaten to interrupt movement of commercial shipping, or against belligerent states that try to break out of their own areas to threaten others. These operations usually take place in areas called "choke points" which typically have:

- no readily available alternate route;

- a waterway of vital importance to one or more nations; and

- a potential aggressor who could close the waterway.

The Strait of Hormuz, the Strait of Gibraltar (200 ships/day), the Strait of Juan de Fuca, the St. Lawrence Seaway, and the Panama Canal are all examples of choke points. Often the trade disruptions would be insufficiently important to have much political value but there are a few points that are critical for the world. Oil is the resource that makes the Strait of Hormuz so vital and any threat to it brings an international response. Now that Iran has submarines....

The opposite to denying passage through choke points is keeping them open and submarines can also do this effectively by monitoring who else is there underwater. Called barrier operations, these are an integral part of the western navies' submarine forces' capabilities.

In wartime, perhaps the submarines greatest role is strategic. Submarines capable of launching nuclear missiles are the ultimate in deterrence--nothing equals this type of latent strike power--and this type of submarine is unquestionably any navy's greatest strategic asset. But they can also provide tactical deterrence when an opposing side threatens escalation in a conflict. Submarines, simply by their suspected presence, can bottle up a surface fleet, as happened in WWII and in the Falklands War. They can force an opposing navy to devote huge amounts of resources to anti-submarine activity, thus depleting their ability to employ their fleet units on other tasks.

Listening and watching, skills that submarines have in spades, advance their surveillance role to the top of the list. In the coming century, this role will also involve more fisheries protection, drug interdiction, prevention of illegal immigration, and pollution control. A submerged submarine is able to approach a vessel engaged in illegal activities undetected and gather information that will allow a nation to take effective legal action. Military force in this type of law enforcement is rarely used and is always a last resort. The submarine's role is simply to gather evidence and to provide a presence as a deterrent, both of which the submarine does superbly. Whether a submarine is actually there or not may be irrelevant--just knowing it *might* be may be enough to deter lawbreakers.

Anti-submarine warfare is an essential role of the submarine in modern navies. Working synergistically with the surface ships and aircraft of the ASW team, the submarine brings its unique characteristics to a difficult art. Ideally positioned and equipped, the submarine can locate other submarines operating at great distances; it can monitor huge areas of ocean or coastal regions; and can gather submarine intelligence for multilateral forces in areas where the opponent has superiority.

Acoustic signature measurement is a little considered but very important role of submarines today. In peacetime, collecting the unique sound characteristics of known vessels enables navies to build up their libraries of sound signatures against which they compare a new contact's sound. This ability to identify a contact is crucial when conflicts arise and a submarine captain needs to know who he is hearing... is it friend or foe?

The provision of targets for ASW fleet training is another vital role of submarines and is one that should not be dismissed because the Cold War has ended. The availability of submarines for training other submarines, surface ships, and aircraft in ASW is fundamental for any navy that plans to be engaged in multilateral operations of a peacekeeping nature.

"Submarines make small navies credible and possible for us to keep our surface fleet relatively small and unsophisticated," commented Vice Admiral Robert Simpson-Anderson, Chief of the South African Navy in 1996.

The international submarine scene is worth knowing about if you are a country engaged in pursuing global peace. Instead of sticking our heads in the sand, let's stick them underwater to see what is going on around the world and what we may have to contend with as peacekeepers. One telling statistic came out in March 1993--while military exports were declining significantly around the world, submarine sales had increased 29%.

"...The major teams are on the wane; the minors are on the move,"[46] observed a senior Canadian submariner in 1991. This is a good place to start our all-round look. In almost all major Western navies, like the US and Britain, submarine numbers and construction has declined since the end of the Cold War. However, in other navies, conventionally-powered submarines have been proliferating since the 1960s and this trend is worrying because some of these nations can be expected to start or join regional conflicts in the 21st century. The world's designers and builders of submarines include Russia, US, France, UK, China, Germany, Australia, North Korea, Sweden, Japan, Turkey, Brazil, and South Korea.

Submarine growth has already taken place in the northwest Pacific, the northern Indian Ocean, and the Mediterranean. The number of conventional boats in the Asia-Pacific region, including

India, is expected to double, and Iran, Taiwan, Malaysia, Thailand, Singapore, the United Arab Emirates, Oman and Saudi Arabia are acquiring submarines for the first time. Eighteen additional countries yearn to operate submarines, and while one might think it takes years for new submariners to become proficient, they learn fast. For example, the Pakistani submarine service sank an Indian frigate in 1971, one year after they first acquired their boats. In 1993 North Korea, China, Sweden, and Russia added new diesel/electric submarines to their fleets.

In the same period, Argentina and Brazil had nuclear submarine programs in financial trouble--it is doubtful if they will be successful, but the desire is there. If they do rustle up the hard cash, both could have SSNs by 2010. In late June 1998, India announced plans to build a fleet of five nuclear powered submarines with the capability of carrying nuclear missiles, with the first one to be completed in 2004. India's desire for nuclear defence stems from her proximity to Pakistan and China, with whom she has fought four wars in the last fifty years.

Vice Admiral G.W. Emery, USN, Commander, Submarine Force, US Atlantic Fleet said that the submarine provides Third World nations with affordable super-power influence. There is no doubt that smaller nations see submarines as part of their counter-intervention forces--rather than retaliating against a dominant country with terrorism, a minor power can use submarines to close choke points, attack shipping, and lay mines, which brings war to the big nation's doorstep without threatening civilians. So it is no wonder that submarines are popular with aggressive countries. Even operating midget submarines and swimmer delivery vehicles can fill the bill and they are much cheaper and can be acquired in greater numbers than regular sized boats.

In 1939, twenty-five navies had submarines, of which only seven were outside Europe. Today forty-four navies around the world operate 740 submarines, of which about 450 are diesel/electric powered (see Appendix 1 for a detailed tally). While a head count, or rather a bow count, tells us something, it does not enlighten us about the capability represented by the hulls. About ninety of the 450 conventional boats are midgets with some very successful special operations under their belts in North Korea and the Middle East; some are old but have had weapons and sensor upgrades that make them very modern, a few have incorporated AIP, and others are obsolescent. Another look at the data tells us that one-third of all the world's submarines (both conventional and nuclear-powered) are operated by Russia, one-third by NATO countries, and the rest by a variety of nations, some of whom are distinctly trigger-happy. (See Appendix 2) Hezbollah, for example, allegedly has twelve one-man submarines. In NATO only Iceland, Belgium and Luxembourg do not operate submarines. The overall balance of submarines and ASW forces varies with the theatre, but it is safe to say that the ASW assets in Western navies have declined. Experts expect that the number of submarines will have dropped to 606 by year 2000 but the capability these boats represent will be greater than the 740.

This proliferation of the conventionally powered submarine puts the focus less on deep ocean operations, which preoccupied submarine services in the Cold War, and more on shallow, coastal operations. Working in shallow water requires a slightly different skill set and smaller, more manoeuvrable boats than the British and Americans have. Canada, with the Victorias arriving in year 2000, will be in a strong position to further develop and provide this type of expertise to the western alliance.

Three decades ago, when nuclear-powered boats were in the ascendancy and the Cold War was at its height, many observers of the submarine community around the world predicted the demise of the diesel/electric submarine. Today we know that prediction was off the mark; they are more popular than ever--growing in numbers, capability, stealth, and are developing new roles. More boats are being built around the world--about 125 more--and several nations anticipate incorporating AIP in their new diesel/electric boats. Most of these new submarines are intended for use in the Pacific and the Indian Oceans. This increase in popularity of diesel/electric submarines is not as puzzling as it first appears. Conventional boats are much more affordable to build, acquire, and operate than nuclear-powered attack submarines; they are very versatile, multi-role vessels for regional navies; they are a strategic asset when used in task groups; there is an increase in civil underwater projects around the world like offshore oil; and they provide enormous bang for the buck. So for small and medium powers the modest investment (comparatively) required for conventional submarines is out of all proportion to the capability they add to their navies and to the level of influence they deliver to their nations' leaders. Many of these are Third World nations and most people believe that any developing country will not have enough submarines to worry about. Well, collectively the Third World operates 200 conventionally powered boats as of year 2000... and it only takes two or three diesel/electric submarines to hold the world to ransom and sink ships.

Before discussing whether a nuclear-powered submarine is better to have than a diesel/electric boat, a word on their differences and nomenclature:

> *"An 'SS' is simply an attack submarine which has no special propulsion configuration or weapons fit. Historically, its prime wartime role has been anti-shipping. Most WWII submarines fit that classification. An 'SSN' is a nuclear-propelled attack submarine, and is usually capable of prosecuting surface vessels and other submarines. Because of its virtually unlimited endurance, high speed capability, and fire-power, the SSN can be considered to be the modern version of the WWI cruiser or battleship...it is, in effect, the modern capital ship. An 'SSBN' is a strategic, nuclear-propelled unit, capable of delivering ballistic missiles. To complicate matters, more than two decades ago, the USSR introduced anti-ship guided (cruise) missiles into their submarine force; that led to the designation "SSG" and later, its reactor-fitted version, the 'SSGN.' Finally, there is the 'SSK,' or poor man's equivalent of the SSN. It is a conventionally propelled submarine which is used primarily in the anti-submarine warfare role, but which can normally be expected to have an anti-surface ship capability."[47]*

Nuclear-powered and diesel/electric submarines have been compared endlessly since the first SSN was launched in 1954, usually to the detriment of the conventional breed. Certainly the British and Americans have long believed that SSNs are beyond compare and any country that could afford nuclear-powered submarines would be stupid not to invest in them. Indeed, as if to highlight the point, both the RN and the USN have chosen to divest themselves of their few remaining conventional boats. The differences lie in their power sources, not in their weapons or sensors, which are often the same.

Advocates of diesel/electric submarines argue their value energetically and continue to point out their advantages. Firstly, conventionally-powered boats are quicker to construct and cheaper to build, acquire, and operate than nukes--about half the amount-- although the expensive weapons fits cost the same. They are still quieter than nuclear-powered submarines, despite quieting technology that has dramatically improved SSNs noise propagation even at higher speeds. Conventional submarines are ideally suited to barrier operations as long as they are based fairly close to the operating area. They are more manoeuvrable as they are generally smaller than the smallest SSN, whose nuclear reactor takes up a lot of space. This smaller size makes conventional submarines better suited to coastal operations in shallow and restricted waters. Automation, which reduces the numbers of crew and thus has an impact on size, is implemented more in diesel/electric submarines.

The disadvantages of diesel/electric submarines lie primarily in their power plants' need for air to replenish their batteries. This requires the submarines to surface or snorkel regularly, which greatly increases their chances of detection. It also means they do not have the sustained high speed that would allow them to deploy rapidly to distant trouble spots or reach distant, fast-moving contacts. Conventional boats certainly get there eventually but their slower, more economical speed delays their arrival, which may degrade their value in certain kinds of operations. Nor can conventionally powered submarines operate under the ice of the Arctic Ocean. For Canada with millions of square kilometers of ice-covered waters, and not only in the Arctic, this is a significant issue, whereas for Spain or Australia, it is not. Diesel boats can certainly operate in the Arctic approaches but, without an air independent power modification, they cannot hope to do more.

Although submariners would have us believe that all types of submarines are perfect, they do have a few limitations whether they are conventionally or nuclear-powered. For example, a submarine is unable to fire a shot across the bows of boat fishing illegally or a drug smuggler trying to evade arrest. Submarines either fire torpedoes to kill or refrain from firing their weapons altogether--they have no middle ground, no graduated response. They compensate for this by either revealing their presence or by calling in a surface vessel, which can provide a more reasonable amount of force necessary to discourage a lawbreaker. Likewise, a submarine does not readily allow the boarding of vessels believed to be carrying contraband or fishing illegally and it usually has to resort to the same solution. When *Ojibwa* was tracking US scallop draggers in 1993 on the Georges Bank, there were concerns that "hostile fishermen could fire weapons at or attempt to ram a [surfaced] submarine and that nets and other fishing gear complicated the problems of submerged movement in a high density fishing area."[48]

From the point of view of carrying troops and equipment, submarines do not project power as effectively as surface vessels. The characteristics that contribute to their stealth also work to limit their ability to detect aircraft and missiles and to maintain tactical communications with their partners in the ASW team. Although a submarine can submerge to avoid most of the threats that beset surface ships, this ability does not make it a viable replacement for them. The two types of vessel are used for different roles, used in different places. Both are necessary; neither can be dispensed with.

Opponents of submarines often use the argument that the seas will soon become transparent, thus wiping out the majority of a submarine's advantages. This predicted transparency is still far from reality as the century turns, even after nearly forty years of dedicated research. Radar, infrared, or blue-green lasers mounted on satellites cannot penetrate the surface of the sea more than a few feet as the water absorbs these wavelengths. Certainly ideas for non-acoustic systems abound and many more are probably out there, but are classified. They include the measurement of surface effects (the miniscule hump on the surface of the ocean pushed up a submarine) or the infrared "scar" that rises to the surface after the passage of a submarine. Unfortunately, these telltale events occur after the submarine has left the area, are not as useful as they might appear, and are easily avoided by an astute submarine captain.

The ideal platforms for many detection systems may seem to be satellites, but they are unlikely to play a role in sub-surface surveillance because they remain limited in their ability to provide real time processing and the presence of clouds still defeats effective monitoring. Also, geostationary orbits are too high above the Earth, at about 35,000 km, to be able to detect small objects like ships or submarines. Nor can satellites provide the continuous coverage of large geographic areas, especially the Polar Regions-- Canadian RADARSAT, for example, has a revisit time of three days. Even if it could see through the clouds and underwater, so many satellites would be required for continual coverage that the system would cost too much--one RADARSAT costs the same as four Victoria class submarines, brand new.

However, it is submarines cost-effectiveness that makes them the favourites of navies world-wide. Costing much less to build than a frigate, they can monitor four times more ocean and bring unique attributes that create balance in fleets dealing with the three-dimensional character of the sea. Modern diesel/electric submarines cost between $250 and $750 million each, depending on their size and complexity. SSNs and frigates cost around $1 billion a copy. Not only do submarines cost less to buy, they cost less to operate--about 60% less than a frigate (see table 2). This indisputable fact is not lost on navies of nations with limited resources and accounts for the proliferation of submarines in the Third World and the increase in submarine exports. Furthermore, countries that have submarines in their inventory of naval vessels also find their industry pursuing new technologies that will pay significant dividends and governments often support the work with research grants and contracts. We see advances in fuel cells, advanced underwater monitoring and survey techniques, data processing and display, and the general development of man's ability to function in extreme environments.

Submarines are special; submarines are unique; and if you have a navy, submarines are indispensable. Their characteristics of stealth, endurance, and cost-effectiveness make them essential to many navies around the world, big and small. Furthermore, their versatility and ability to provide influence politically and diplomatically is undeniable. But it is in the area of surveillance that they reign supreme amongst capital ships.

Chapter Nine
CANADA NEEDS SUBMARINES

Twenty hours out from Halifax, HMCS *Ojibwa*, arrived on station. She dived unseen. The submarine was close to the Hague Line, an imaginary line drawn between the Canadian and American scallop beds on the Georges Bank in the Atlantic ocean. The US stocks had been depleted through over fishing but the Canadian ones, well regulated, were healthy, productive, and very tempting--one night's poaching could net 5,000 lbs. American scallop draggers were hovering close to the line waiting for darkness. *Ojibwa* sighted and identified her first contact through the periscope at 2010. Using her passive sonar *Ojibwa* started to track the vessel at about 4,000 yards. The American boat stayed on the US side. Another did not. This one, tracked and identified, could not be apprehended, as some equipment failed at the wrong moment and *Ojibwa* could not provide the evidence necessary for court proceedings. A few days later, having maintained a very close eye on the straying vessel, *Ojibwa* saw it and one other move into Canadian waters. The DFO officer on board radioed the two fish boats and told them that they had been tracked for several days by a Canadian submarine, and if they crossed the Hague Line again, they would be apprehended and charged. Within moments the US scallop draggers had informed all US fish boats in the area that a Canadian submarine on patrol was watching them. The Canadian fishers were delighted at the submarine's intervention because they believed that about $1 million in revenue was being lost each month to foreign poaching.[49]

The defence review process in 1994 heard loud and clear that few nations have as conspicuous a need for a sub-surface capability as Canada; in fact the need can be traced back to the beginnings of the RCN when formal stated submarine requirements appeared soon after submarines were introduced into service. In 1912 and 1918, they were seen as vital for Canada--in both British Admiralty reviews submarines were recommended for the Atlantic and Pacific in a coastal defence capacity. U-boats had ventured across the pond by the end of WWI and our first boats, *CC1* and *CC2*, were pressed into service for the some of the world's earliest passive sonar experiments with Alexander Graham Bell in 1918.[50] Since then submarines have threatened or directly attacked Canada four times and, in most instances, we had none of our own to counter them.

More recently, in 1983, the Senate Sub-committee of Defence recommended seventeen coastal submarines to replace the Oberon submarines. By 1987, Canada had moved to twelve nuclear-powered submarines. In 1992, the defence policy brought the requirement back down to six diesel/electric boats and in 1998 we acquired only four. Public support for submarines has varied widely during this period because most Canadians do not understand why we should have them. In Feb 1997, the Pollara poll indicated that 60% of Canadians were in favour of replacing the O boats, but by November, the Southam News/COMPAS poll showed a vastly different level of support--only 7% endorsed submarines. However, it must be said that the two polls had different emphases--the first was solely on defence, the second focused on government spending.

Today the Canadian navy believes that Canada must retain our submarine service because:

- There have been marked increases in challenges to Canadian sovereignty;

- There have been more encroachments into Canadian waters in an increasingly resource-poor world;

- here is less strategic stability in the world;

- Global security is volatile; and

- There is an ever-changing void in the world's power structure since the end of the Cold War.

The concept of submarine operations in Canada for this century[51] requires submarine capabilities that are primarily defensive in nature. The majority of the work for Canadian submarines from the year 2000 onward, presuming that we remain at peace, will mirror the navy's, outlined in their recent planning documents. It will revolve around surveillance and control in support of Canadian security, a capability and credibility in ASW in support of multilateral operations, training in sub-surface warfare of our ships and aircraft, and leverage with our allies for intelligence and information sharing. But we must remember that these defensive skills are interchangeable with offensive.

In 1994, the Special Joint Committee, when reviewing Canadian defence requirements, started out opposed to continuing our submarine service. By the time their work concluded the committee members had changed their minds and recommended its retention. These civilians did their homework, listened carefully, and learned very quickly that our navy cannot do without its sub-surface component.

The committee realized that submarines are the main instruments of sovereignty for medium powers due to their value, stealth, and endurance. They learned the proof supporting the premise--forty-nine countries world wide operate submarines, as well as most NATO nations. They discovered that few of those countries are facing a direct threat--they in fact use their submarines mainly for sovereignty purposes. They also heard about the Australian example--the RAN is rebuilding their navy around submarines... and they have neither ice nor a direct threat. In fact, at the end of the 20th century there was no evidence to suggest that submarines will lose their place as the capital ship of choice for most navies.

The best way to explain our need for submarines is to look at each commitment the government has made in its current defence and foreign policies and see how submarines apply to them. Then we need to consider the value they add to our navy.

First and foremost, Canada's defence policy articulates the need for the protection of our sovereignty. After the collapse of the Warsaw Pact, the need to monitor foreign submarines in our maritime areas certainly diminished, but the need to be able to effectively monitor our territorial seas began to grow. Some of the reasons for this growth included the measurable increase in encroachments into our waters and the greater demands placed on maritime nations by the UN Convention on the Law of the Sea. Submarines, with their unique attributes, are ideal platforms for surveillance of Canada's vast open ocean areas and our new Victorias, with an AIP retrofit, should be able to operate under the ice in a few years. Modern submarines can monitor activity in much of Canada's 11 million square kilometers of ocean, a claim that the surface ships cannot make. We already have striking examples of how a submarine on patrol can effectively reduce illegal fishing and how it can covertly gather evidence in narcotics smuggling--activities that every Canadian wishes to stop, or at least curtail.

The analysis of Operation Ambuscade in 1993 (when HMCS *Ojibwa* was deployed to catch US scallop draggers violating the Hague Line on the Georges Bank) highlighted the value of a submarine in sovereignty protection of this type, as well as cooperation between other government departments. The Department of Fisheries and Oceans (DFO) compared the use of a Canadian submarine with other methods:

Helicopters had some 'covert capability' but had limited range and endurance and were weather dependent. Patrol vessels could stay on station, manoeuvre, and send out boarding parties--but they were not covert, and again, there were weather limitations. Though submarines had limitations--for example, their primary strength precluded them from apprehension--DFO concluded that 'no other

DFO platform has the ability to covertly track, locate, identify, and monitor vessels in fog.' In addition, DFO did not have the capability to 'obtain the distinctive acoustic signatures of fishing vessels.'[52]

The fact that Canada operates submarines to support Fisheries and Oceans was made well known following this operation and the number of US violations of the Hague Line dropped from thirty-three in 1993 to one in 1995. There is no doubt that AMBUSCADE saved millions of dollars worth of fish stocks and proved that war-fighting skills are applicable to law enforcement situations. Submarines, in this instance, do even better when operating with aircraft and DFO recommended that they introduce a 'sub-air' concept on the Hague Line. As in anti-submarine warfare, maritime patrol aircraft and submarines make excellent partners in fisheries protection and enforcement. Aircrews can alert a dived submarine to concentrations of fishing vessels in contentious areas and the submarine can then undertake covert surveillance where it counts most. Furthermore, as a submarine may identify other vessels by their emitted noise and through the periscope, it is a very effective "cueing" platform for aircraft and surface ships--for example, submarines can call in a surface ship to board a vessel believed to have been fishing illegally.

When the Oberons were upgraded in the 1980s, their new sensors increased their detection ranges, as well as improving their capability of classifying contacts. In 1983, the boats began to conduct operational surveillance patrols in the Atlantic for the first time. Their success in learning about the activity in our own maritime backyard convinced the navy of the submarines' value--three boats and less than 300 submariners had assisted the maritime team paint a clearer picture of the activities of friendly and not so friendly nations in our territorial waters. The impact of this knowledge was huge, especially considering that the submarine squadron used only a tiny percentage of the navy's annual budget.

New Canadian submarines will minimize future threats to our sovereignty from illegal fishing, drug running, and illegal immigration. Their deterrent value is linked to their stealth. It is easier for a vessel acting illegally to cope with six frigates whose positions are known than one submarine whose position is not known. Submarines show that Canada means business and they strengthen our diplomatic positions and strategies.

Underestimating the value of submarines in peacetime for sovereignty protection is a national pastime. However, we must remember that their psychological impact is significant: "They're like a radar trap. You never know whether they're around or not, which makes you think twice. During the turbot confrontation with Spain, intercepted radio messages from the Spanish trawlers show they were spotting periscopes in the water. There was never actually a sub in the region."[53]

Our submarines work with a surprising number of other government departments in the interests of Canada--from the advancement of science and technology to law enforcement. They assist in research for the civilian, industrial, and military sectors, often in less accessible areas like the Arctic Archipelago. Submarines can be found working with immigration, fisheries, our police agencies, and the department of the environment, as well as attending disasters at sea (e.g. *Okanagan* after Swiss Air flight 111 crashed near Peggy's Cove, NS.). The submarine enforces others to comply with the law by possibly being there.

In the matter of continental defence, submarines also play their part. Just as our navy cooperates with the US navy in the joint protection of the North American continent, as laid down in our defence policy and by joint treaties, so do our submarines. Canada is responsible for maritime areas of the Atlantic and Pacific that lie outside our EEZ but in defence terms come under our jurisdiction in the continental scheme of things. Canada has committed to monitor activity above and below the sea and to protect shipping in:

- The northwest Atlantic, related to the movement of shipping between North America and Europe;

- The northeast Pacific, including the Strait of Juan de Fuca, the northern approaches to BC, and up and down the coast to/from Alaska; and,

- The Arctic, related to detection of submarines passing through the Arctic Archipelago.

Long after the Cold War ended and after most of us thought the former Soviet navy had ceased to be of concern, Russian SSNs were discovered roaming close to US submarine bases and monitoring the American SSBNs. This activity escalated as recently as 1995 and demonstrated Canada still has an underwater job to do in her Atlantic and Pacific treaty-assigned jurisdictions. We cannot be complacent about this type of activity and we cannot monitor it effectively without submarines.

Strategically the Arctic is crucially important, not only to the western alliance but also to Canada, because the Arctic Ocean provides access to any ocean of the world and is a good place to hide submarines. Control of access to North America via the Arctic has provided Canada with substantial leverage for decades, and is thought to be key to Canada's ability to act as a sovereign nation within the CAN/US defence relationship, dominated as it is by the United States.[54]

Some observers even go so far as to say that if Canada can retain this level of Arctic leverage it will help prevent our assimilation by the United States. Additionally, Canada's assertion of sovereignty over the North West Passage increases our voice in multilateral Arctic talks and defence agreements. Continuance of this leverage is dependent upon Canada retaining an ability to control the Arctic approaches and the waters of the Arctic Archipelago which we claim as internal. The ever-present ice and the fact that it is usually only submarines that transit through this region means Canada has no choice but to operate submarines to uphold our position and influence continentally.

Foreign submarines that are under-ice capable can use the Arctic to move between the Pacific and Atlantic oceans because it is a shorter route than going round Cape Horn or the Cape of Good Hope. However, it is a very arduous passage and only US boats have been known to use it. As NATO effectively controls the choke point known as the GIUK* gap, an alternative is for

*Greenland, Iceland, United Kingdom.

submarines to use the route through the Davis Strait between Greenland and Canada, which falls under our responsibility. Furthermore, as the Canadian Arctic waters make up nearly half the maritime territory for which Canada has or claims to have responsibility--5.4 million sq. kms (MAP#2)--our need to exert our sovereignty in the Arctic is pressing for environmental and resource reasons as well. This is not something that is easy to accomplish in the most hostile climate in the world.

Canada presently has three Arctic and Maritime Surveillance Aircraft (CP-140A *Arcturus*), which carry out above-water surveillance in the Arctic. Of course, the ice cover limits their utility. To monitor activity under the ice effectively requires sub-surface operations. Fixed sonar systems can be useful if specially designed and can detect any submarines that pass through but do not allow a response. In the ice-covered approaches to the Arctic, fixed systems have design challenges to overcome that they do not have in the open ocean and have proven too costly at this time. With nuclear-powered submarines a no-go for Canada, the new fleet of Victorias will have to be modified with air-independent power (AIP) to gain access to the high Arctic, where the ice prevents their ability to recharge their batteries. This advanced technology is proven in Germany, Sweden, and soon to be in Canada, but it is not fully tried yet. The Department of National Defence has not articulated how many AIP capable boats would be required to perform this role adequately in such a vast northern area.

Canada did plan to utilize fixed underwater acoustic arrays in the Arctic Archipelago. However, the Arctic Subsurface Surveillance System (ARCSSS) died when an effective, reasonably priced system could not be found and few submarines were thought to use this difficult route. In the future, if a system is developed that Canada can afford DND may consider it. However, there is no relationship between the loss of the ARCSSS and the acquisition of the Victoria submarines, as some commentators have surmised.

Additionally Canada has obligations to our NATO allies, who expect us to maintain a certain degree of naval readiness and capability. Submarines help Canada and our navy to pull our weight with our allies by:

- Participating in multilateral task groups;

- Providing our major allies, Britain and the US, with diesel/electric submarines for ASW training, which hopefully will allow us to generate revenue that is impossible with any other naval asset;

- Providing a capability for shallow water operations and training; and,

- Participating in waterspace management.

Canada's submarines also provide the means to perform barrier operations. These traditionally were expected to take place in the choke points where Soviet submarines might pass from their northern ports through to the open Atlantic but the threat has lessened for the time being.

However, there is no reason why Canadian submarines could not be used for barrier operations elsewhere in the world--our allies may expect Canadian submarines to be available to control access anywhere multilateral operations take place in the future including, and maybe most especially, in the north Pacific. If a task force is engaged in barrier operations submarines can take the lead, enter the choke point if the waters appear to be controlled by an adversary, or can rid the area of dangers. If the area is not occupied, submarines can provide advanced warnings to its task force of approaching threats.

International sanctions, embargoes, and blockades are meaningless unless they are properly enforced. International organizations or countries commonly impose these punishments to reprimand nations for behaving improperly, engaging in conflicts, or to cut off military supplies to warring factions. Submarines can play their parts in these activities by monitoring surface activity and alerting surface ships when they find a vessel acting suspiciously or trying to run a blockade with forbidden cargo.

Peacekeeping is the last role of the Canadian Forces stated in both our defence and foreign policies--we are renowned for our willingness to participate in far-flung conflicts. With the expectations that the world will remain unstable and that Canada will continue to uphold her obligations in this direction, our government will send our navy to hot spots regularly, and often before our army and air force. The need of submarines may or may not be necessary every time but when they are, the Victorias could perform several vital tasks if they can be spared from home. They could monitor opposing submarine activity and respond to the threat it poses to the allied forces; perform surveillance duties for the multilateral task groups, especially in areas where the opposing forces have air superiority; gather intelligence or take part in special operations; provide sea control and denial like blockades; assist in enforcing sanctions; and work in shallow coastal areas where nukes do not go. Submarines, in medium intensity conflicts, provide a large measure of security for the surface forces, protecting them from enemy submarines and allowing them to stay out of heavily defended forward areas. The presence or suspected presence of submarines doubles an opponent's need for ships and aircraft and keeps them occupied.

In the greater scheme of things, submarines, whether Canadian or not, are useful deterrents in peacekeeping operations because they keep opposing fleets cooped up and away from the coalition forces. We also need to bear in mind that the Russians have been unloading submarines to any interested takers, so it no longer takes a rogue regime ten years to develop a submarine force. They can be ready to go in two--a significant reason for Canada to maintain submariners and expertise as well as hulls.

Submarines also support Canada's foreign policy. Diplomacy as a role for submarines is difficult for landlubbers to understand, but it exists in their participation in joint exercises, port visits, operational training, and peacekeeping missions. The importance of controlling access to the Arctic waters has far-reaching strategic and political implications as previously discussed. The Arctic leverage which Canada has maintained for decades, albeit somewhat tenuously, is important to this nation remaining sovereign and resisting assimilation by the USA. It also provides us with more voice in international defence discussions. There are few vessels that can effectively exercise sovereignty in our north like a submarine can--as long as it is equipped for under-ice operations--and this fact has not escaped our politicians, even if it has escaped most of the rest of us.

Nations who have attempted to steal fish in our territorial waters, or perhaps have just thought about it, learned the diplomatic value of submarines when Canada negotiated with Spain and the European Union after the Turbot War. The possibility of a Canadian submarine on the fishing grounds photographing their ships in the act of poaching, gave Canada a very strong advantage at the bargaining table. Our new submarines, especially one on the west coast, will undoubtedly aid the very tough negotiations with the US over salmon in the north-west Pacific as the Alaskan fishing fleet refuses to take measures to conserve the precious fish stocks.

Having seen how submarines fit into the Canadian defence and foreign policies, it is now time to articulate the value they add to our navy. One of the most important reasons that Canada needs to have submarines is for the maintenance of ASW proficiency. Many people would have the Canadian public believe that anti-submarine warfare and maritime surveillance are different; that they need completely different platforms and skills. These individuals also say since we do not have to deal with submarine threats at home any more, we no longer need to worry much about ASW. This misguided opinion leads directly to their proposition to get rid of our submarines. It is a fashionable route to an assumption that is quite erroneous, and if acted upon, has very serious implications for our sovereignty protection in this century. **For it is the ASW skills themselves, that provide the Canadian navy with their maritime surveillance abilities**.

It is the ability to use sophisticated sonar and other sensors to their maximum potential to monitor our ocean areas. It is the ability to prevail within the ever-changing acoustic properties of the seas, especially in shallow, restricted waters where sound propagation is so difficult to predict. It is the ability to collect and classify acoustic signatures. It is the ability to remain current with the advances in sensor technology. It is the ability to develop, maintain, and improve the skills of the sensors' operators.

Maritime Command constantly hones all these ASW/surveillance skills and applies them directly, not only to our submarines, but also to our surface ships and aircraft, thus developing an effective ASW team and task group. This is the only way we can effectively monitor our vast ocean areas, as well as safely participate in peacekeeping missions. And above all, it means practising... and practising... and practising. All three together!

Maintaining ASW proficiency for submariners means they maintain their ability to fully appreciate a total "surveillance picture." This is a difficult underwater art, as well as a science, and relates to the ability to use passive sensors, such as sonar, and not rely on active sensors like radar, which may give them away. It means learning how to meld into surroundings to become invisible while detecting and monitoring the activity of others. It means knowing the vagaries of ocean acoustics in their patrol areas and knowing whom they are hearing. It means being intuitive and creative. It means developing a sixth sense to predict what the contact will do next. And above all, it means practising so they do not lose the critical edge which marks the difference between competence and incompetence, and perhaps life and death.

Had Canada decided submarines were an anachronism, our navy would have been left with nothing underwater, one third of our surveillance team would have disappeared, the ability to train the team effectively would have been lost, and there would be no hope of monitoring activity below our ice-covered waters. In the larger perspective, we would also have lost our submarine service-- something akin to losing our naval aviation component.

As the Canadian navy has the reputation of being extremely good at ASW, we can safely extrapolate that they are very good at surveillance as well. However, if they lose that ability, it would take at least a generation to restore it--about twenty years. It is not just the tactical aspects that would be difficult to recover, but it would be relearning how to operate submarines and sonars that presents a challenge too.

ASW is a complex and perishable skill. All navies face challenges in this area of expertise as never before--both quiet SSNs and SSKs with AIP can be almost impossible to detect acoustically in poor conditions. The modern conventional submarine is one of the most potent threats coalition surface forces face, especially in shallow coastal waters like the Persian Gulf where they can go undetected for days at a time despite the best equipment and personnel trying to find them. With the proliferation of smaller diesel/electric boats in the risky regions of the world, Maritime Command has no choice but to ensure the navy's ASW capability is first rate. So we see that ASW is not dead, but alive and kicking. Task groups must be ready for shallow water ASW, which was less prevalent during the Cold War years and is difficult to do well. There is a very real danger that if we fail to realize its importance and do not train for it, lives could be lost abroad just as they were in WWII.

Now that we understand the link between ASW skills and those needed for surveillance, we can discuss ASW training in the knowledge of its expanded meaning to the Canadian navy of the 21st century. Historically Canada acquired submarines to train their surface fleet and aircrews in anti-submarine warfare; indeed that was the primary reason that the Oberon class boats were bought in the 1960s.

Today the recent submarine acquisition is more for surveillance and sovereignty protection reasons than ASW, so a better name for ASW training might be SASW--surveillance and anti-submarine warfare training (or even ASS--anti-submarine and surveillance!). This role will be a very important one for the Victorias to undertake, for their own sakes and those of our ships and aircraft. All three platforms must maintain these skills at the highest level for sovereignty protection and against the time when they are abroad on multilateral operations in submarine threatened areas. Also, the submarines themselves must continue their own submarine-versus-submarine training exercises.

Furthermore, the USN's lack of diesel/electric submarines to train with is troubling them considerably. As the majority of submarines Americans meet in multilateral operations are conventional, they are seeking diesel/electric boats from their allies for ASW training purposes, as well as for shallow water training. With Britain also out of the conventional game, the US is looking to Canada to supply SSKs and has already offered money to use our new Victorias. There are sound reasons for Canada to provide this service, not the least of which are our traditions of cooperation with our allies and the experience it gives our submariners. The other reason, and perhaps the most attractive, is the prospect of earning some revenue to offset the operating costs of the new boats. However, the US need is so great these days that the new

Canadian Victorias may just end up *making* money in the early years of the 21st century--a novel idea for any defence department.

Minelaying*, mine countermeasures, reconnaissance before special operations, and protection of amphibious forces and shipping are other tasks submarines can perform in multilateral undertakings. They take place in the littoral or coastal seas of maritime nations which are characterized by difficult
acoustic properties, high traffic density, and much ambient noise. Shallow water operations require special expertise that navies allowed to decline during the Cold War. The recent de-emphasis of ASW further magnifies the losses in shallow ASW skills.
Diesel/electric boats are superb at this kind of work--remaining incredibly hard to detect without resorting to active sonar and still being able to deliver deterrence and damage to surface vessels. With Britain and the US out of diesel/electric boats, Canada is one nation and senior NATO partner that will continue to have submarines that can perform well in coastal areas. Our submarine service, long adept in deep ocean ASW, is also good in shallow waters and it plans to become even better in this field. As they do so, the Canadians will be much in demand for training purposes, certainly by the USN, who needs the experience for domestic reasons like Canada's, as well as for distant operations against countries who operate diesel/electric boats exclusively.

Submarines, including the new Victorias, are often described as Cold War relics that have only offensive roles. They are much more versatile than that, as we have seen. Canada has never used submarines in anti-ship roles, although they carry torpedoes, but the capability will be there, as it was with the Oberons.

Canada shares sub-sea intelligence with our allies who also operate submarines. Britain and US not only tell us where their submarines are operating, but where Chinese, Russian, and others' boats are too. This information aids in underwater accident prevention, prevents mutual interference during patrols and exercises, as well as provides us with knowledge of how other nations are using their boats. Only if Canada has submarines do we

---

*Canadian submarines have never carried mines and the new Victorias will not either.

participate in this information net, so maintaining a submarine capability preserves the flow of subsea intelligence from other submarine-operating allies. However, at the moment this "waterspace management," as it is called, occurs only on the east coast where our present submarines operate--we get relatively little information or intelligence about foreign submarine activity on the west coast. A Victoria class boat at Esquimalt will change this. Opponents to a Canadian Submarine Service argue that underwater sensors, radars, land-based radio monitoring systems, frigates, and aircraft can gather sufficient information on foreign ship movements for our purposes. The fact is, in many cases, they are not as good at monitoring submarine movements as a submarine. A lack of submarines means that Canada would lose the underwater segment of her surveillance picture--rather like a deaf person listening to a symphony.

Canada has not operated submarines in the Pacific for twenty-five years despite our growing interests in the Asia-Pacific region, the growing power of Asian countries, the growth of submarines in Asian navies, the increasing unrest in parts of the Far East, and the lack of collective security agreements in the region. The area is much bigger than the north Atlantic and is increasingly unstable. Submarines will improve the balance and strength in our west coast fleet, which will give Canada a little more clout in any discussions within the region, whether they concern mutual security arrangements, naval exercises, or peacekeeping if it becomes necessary.

Much more alarming to most Canadians is Vancouver's rise into top spot as the main port of entry in North America for narcotics from the Far East, as well as the arrival of three rusting migrant ships that landed 599 illegal migrants from China in northern BC in 1999. Furthermore, drug and immigrant smugglers relish the ease the uninhabited nature of the Pacific Northwest coast gives their illicit trade. Customs and excise officers and western police forces therefore eagerly anticipate a submarine presence on the west coast.

Soon after year 2000, the Canadian Pacific fleet, larger and more modern than ever before, will at last have a real submarine for its task group and to provide the ongoing underwater surveillance/ASW training they must have. The single Victoria will go partway to fill the hole that the navy in Esquimalt has struggled with since Rainbow paid-off in 1974.

Unfortunately, terrorism has always been with us; indeed, it exists in Canada. We can hardly believe it, but in the period from 1960 to 1985, authorities identified sixteen terrorist groups that were responsible for 341 unlawful incidents. It is a way weaker but aggressive nations (or political arms of ideological organizations) can respond to bullying by a large antagonist. Terrorism can be conducted deep in the heart of the antagonist's nation and inflict great damage to property and civilians. Maritime terrorism is less visible but nevertheless exists and can include piracy, hijacking of ships, kidnapping of crews, and violent protests about cargoes, etc. For example, in the 1970s, Colonel Ghadaffi, the Libyan leader, planned to sink the QE2 when she was carrying American Jews to Israel. Thankfully, he failed. The Royal Navy, the United States Navy, and the Royal Australian Navy already play a major role in international maritime counter-terrorism using the submarine's stealth in deterring and countering such acts. Canada may choose to do the same with the new Victorias.

Other benefits accrue to Canada if our navy operates submarines. While national security requirements come before the need for industrial/regional benefits (IRBs) and jobs, our present submarine force does represent $10 million/year of shipyard business along with the jobs involved. The arrival of the new Victorias will not only preserve this submarine expertise and the jobs that exist now, but may also create new jobs over the thirty-year lifespan of the boats. If the submarine service were disbanded, all of these would be lost.

If the Department of National Defence was a job creation agency, perhaps Canada should consider building our own submarines. A premium always has to be paid to create an industry that is non-existent, and in the case of submarines, Canada would be looking at about $5 billion to design and construct four boats equivalent to the Victorias. Clearly, the jobs such a program would create are out of proportion to the outlay required in this era of tight fiscal policies. The trade-off, however, is less self-reliance.

Opportunities in research and development abound these days. Submarines contribute to ocean science and the development of new marine technologies and, heaven knows, as we are one of the largest maritime nations in the world, we should be at the forefront. The design and construction of remotely operated submersibles for military and commercial purposes and the development of fuel cells for air-independent power systems have partly come about as result of owning and operating submarines. It will surprise many Canadians that Canada leads the world in these two industries and has state of the art facilities for both in southern British Columbia.

Another reason Canada needed new submarines was the age of Canada's three Oberon class submarines, which came into service in the mid- to late-sixties and all of which were in service until 1998 when two were paid off. With a life expectancy of twenty-five years, their useful lives should have been over at the beginning of the nineties. The O boats had been kept alive since 1991 by some of the best submarine maintenance teams in the world, by regular upgrading, and with careful examinations to determine their ability to dive safely. It was an expensive process and, although it certainly kept them operational in an increasingly technological age, time eventually caught up with them. In the last decade the Oberons lost their competitive edge, despite valiant efforts to make them as quiet as possible. Today the Russian Kilo class is quieter and is available on the open arms market.

Without submarines, Canada would have lost an indispensable component of our balanced maritime forces. The costs for sovereignty patrols and other tasks would have escalated through having to increase the use of surface vessels and patrol aircraft, not to mention the distinct possibility of having to buy more assets to offset the deficiency. Effective surveillance would have been compromised. We would have lost access to underwater surveillance data in the Atlantic obtained because we are an operator of submarines in that region. We would have lost the submarine knowledge and skills that have been so painstakingly acquired over the last thirty years. But much more critically, the navy would not have been able to carry out its mandate if Canada had disbanded our submarine service. Now we can look forward to:

- Exercising underwater sovereignty;

- Exercising Arctic sovereignty in the future, with all that implies;

- Conducting effective surface and sub-surface surveillance;

- Training effectively in surveillance/ASW and shallow water operations;

- Participating credibly in multilateral operations on the surface, in the air, and underwater.

Submarines can perform a number of tasks for the nation that no other naval vessel can. The primacy of surveillance and control, reiterated in recent defence department policy documents, has increased the value and need for submarines in the 21st century for Canada, rather than the opposite, without diminishing the requirement for participation of our navy in overseas operations. Submarine roles today may differ from those of the Cold War but the exact same skills are required to perform them.

Stealth, endurance, and invulnerability were the key to submarines' value ninety years ago and remain so today. Canada needs those attributes in our navy as never before to uphold our foreign and defence policies at home and abroad.

Chapter 10
THE CANADIAN SUBMARINE DEBATE

The debate between those for and against submarines has always been heated, and although it has garnered a lot of ink at times, it has been a debate between minorities--the navy and the peace lobby. There is no middle ground between them and the debate is difficult to analyze because the participants sometimes compare apples and oranges; they bring motherhood issues into the picture and they make points based on misinformation, sometimes unintentionally, often deliberately delivered. The majority of Canadians neither cares to participate nor follows the arguments. Some of the contentious issues have already been discussed but there are more to visit.

One commentary going the rounds is that Canada is acquiring four British Upholder submarines because they are a bargain. Yes, the negotiated contract could be interpreted as a bargain, but to believe that Canada is buying them *just* because they are a bargain is completely fallacious. As the preceding two chapters demonstrate, Canada's navy needs submarines to do their job properly for the next three decades.

Submarine opponents often point their fingers to other western submarine fleets and ask, "Why does Canada need submarines if the Brits and Americans are reducing theirs?" Well, in the first place, both those nations had large numbers of submarines during the Cold War. Canada didn't. The USN and the RN were able to reduce the numbers of their operational submarines after the Berlin Wall fell and still have enough for national security purposes and peacekeeping requirements. Canada, in contrast, had only four from the mid-60s to 1974 and three from then to the present, which were insufficient for the navy's mission--probably we needed a minimum of eight during the Cold War. For solely geographic reasons at the turn of the millennium, we could do with a minimum of six, three on each coast, to use for sovereignty protection alone.

Project Ploughshares, one of the loudest opponents and the one who gets most of the ink, believes that the only real value of submarines lies in their war-fighting role. Undoubtedly, that is one of their roles, but it should be clear by now that they are useful for more than that. Fisheries and Oceans certainly think so, for one. In fact, it was considered old fashioned at the end of the 20th century to believe that submarines can do nothing but sink ships. Their fighting skills are the same as those used for the surveillance required in sovereignty protection, as OPERATION AMBUSCADE proved.

Ploughshares also argues that our allies can provide submarines in war to protect us and our interests, if push comes to shove. They say that the British and US boats are better than ours anyway and can outclass any conceivable threat, and also from a war-fighting perspective, that our frigates and aircraft should be enough protection. Historically, Canada has relied on allies for submarines, most notably in WWII, and on each occasion has been quickly disappointed. There is no reason to believe this would change, despite the best intentioned of friends. The lesson here is about the importance of preparedness and independence. Neither are our frigates and aircraft enough if there is another general war or high intensity regional conflict in which our navy is involved. They are too vulnerable to attack from the air and underwater and need submarines to spearhead offensives in areas controlled by the enemy.

Submarines may be quintessential weapons of war but they are also crucial to the total surveillance picture due to their inherent covertness. If we want to know what is going on in our water column, we have to have something in our water column. The submarine gives us that kind of surveillance, whether an intruder is there or not. Regarding the Arctic, Canada has to do more work towards the surveillance and management of resources in that area. Undersea detectors, also known as fixed arrays, only tell you who or what *was* there. You then need to have an ability to respond to that intrusion, otherwise you might as well not know who was there.[55] Rear Admiral Jim King, CD, put it this way, "...in terms of basic protection, basic surveillance, and control (being able to do something), there is nothing that approaches the modern submarine. Nothing!"[56]

To those that say the submarine threat disappeared with the Cold War, the current figures show that submarines are proliferating around the world and countries that have never operated submarines before are now. Some of these nations are distinctly unsavoury and we may find ourselves facing off against them in future multilateral operations.

Opponents of the submarine service say that Canada does not need submarines for training purposes because we can borrow boats from our allies. Unfortunately, our two major allies operate only nuclear-propelled submarines and we need both types with which to train. With the diesel/electric boat again in the ascendant, Canada's navy needs more time working with those, especially if our government continues to send our navy on peacekeeping missions. Certainly Britain and the US could and will provide the Canadian fleet with opportunities to train with their nukes, but where would we find diesel/electric boats with which to practice? The submarine opponents have not answered that question satisfactorily. Possibly we could make arrangements with the Royal Australian (but they are not ready yet) or a European navy but the rental cost would be high and the availability would be at the convenience of the supplying nation. Experience also shows us that usually the supply is too little, too late. Worse yet, if the world order deteriorated drastically, the supplier would want their boats back, just when we needed them most. Historically Canada has tried to rent training boats--both during and after WWII. Both arrangements were unsatisfactory and led to a dependence on another nation. Most importantly, the outcome relating to ASW skills was disappointing, especially in WWII.

Many uninformed individuals think that submarines are a little heavy-handed for controlling illegal fishing and drug running. If submarines had no other role, it could be said that they are overkill in such operations, but for nations with tight purse strings, catching fish poachers and narcotics traffickers is a sensible way of using a unique asset and it provides excellent opportunities for maintaining our vital ASW skills. Those who contend that frigates and aircraft alone can perform these duties need consider the importance of the covert capabilities which can enhance these duties and can best be provided by a sub-surface platform in the frequent low-visibility encountered on the fishing grounds.

A growing number of Canadians truly believe that satellites can assume almost all the surveillance duties Canada needs. This is simply not true. Even if Canada had enough satellites, which we don't and which we could never afford, their sensors cannot penetrate cloud cover or the ocean surface for more than a few feet. Nor can satellites board fish boats or arrest drug runners. This lack of ability to respond to sovereignty infractions means we would still need to have surface assets, though probably more of them.

Several groups, like Canada 21 with members of Parliament on their rosters, have published the view that as the threat from eastern bloc submarines has vanished, our navy does not need submarines to hunt submarines anymore. They want to abandon our navy's anti-submarine warfare role and proceed from there to getting rid of our submarine component altogether. This is a very dangerous suggestion, if only from the simplistic viewpoint that our surface fleet would not have submarines to train with for peacekeeping missions and Canadian crews would have to do their jobs at much greater risk.[57] But what these individuals have completely failed to appreciate is that *all* surveillance skills derive from ASW skills.

Canadian Senator Colin Kenny, originally opposed to submarines, maintains, "We know from experience the vulnerability of our sea links to submarines. Submarines remain one of the greatest threats we would face if tensions, confrontation, or even war return. And that threat, distant as it may be today, could re-emerge much faster than we could re-develop submarine skills if we let them disappear....We must maintain a readiness to respond to a renewed military threat. In the meantime, submarines help protect our sovereignty and can be used to support UN ops."

Others, in the belief that our navy is still built around hunting submarines, feel that our frigates can do the job adequately as long as they get replacement shipborne helicopters. It is those, who have failed to follow the transition of the Canadian navy from meeting primarily NATO requirements to meeting Canadian maritime security needs that have perpetuated this opinion.

Some use the argument that world-wide spending on defence is dropping, so we should drop our defence budget further by excluding submarines from the fleet. Two points spring to mind to rebut this. First, Canadian defence has been seriously neglected for so long that we have been forced into modernizing and augmenting our fleet all at once. Second, the one segment of defence spending that has been rising around the world is for diesel/electric submarines--more than 125 boats were under construction in 1995 and over 700 submarines of all types were at sea. This should be a source of concern to nations who participate in peacekeeping missions at sea.

We hear that submarines are not needed to patrol our coastal waters because our frigates, our new coastal defence vessels, and our maritime patrol aircraft can do it well enough, along with vessels belonging to other government departments. It must be clear by now that ships, planes, and submarines all do different things and are all necessary to meet our coastal security interests. The unique attributes of submarines are essential to augment the others' characteristics and to protect the shores, straits, islands, and resources of the largest maritime domain in the world.

Project Ploughshares would like Canadians to believe the submarine fisheries patrol conducted in 1993 by HMCS *Ojibwa* was a propaganda stunt to justify the acquisition of submarines. Their alternate suggestion was to disguise a trawler to spy on foreign fish boats at a fraction of the cost. *Ojibwa's* patrol was not a stunt and the subsequent behaviour of foreign fishing fleets has since proved that, beyond all question. Furthermore, the US Navy has also successfully used their submarines in similar ways, especially in drug interdiction.

A school of thought does not support submarines being used to monitor embargoes of the UN type because proponents say that surface ships do it better. These ships, they say, are able to board, fire warning shots across the bows of uncooperative vessels, and provide a defusing presence. The truth is there are times when *only* submarines can conduct embargoes. In the Adriatic the embargo was close to a shore where there were Serbian missile emplacements threatening anything that might move on the surface, so the allied submarines had to identify the suspect vessels and alert the surface naval ships to intercept them out of harm's way.

Many Canadians feel that we no longer have a requirement to patrol our Arctic waters, for there is no longer a threat up there. Indeed, they can cite public announcements such as President Clinton's of November 1997 which stated that the US was phasing out SSN patrols under the Arctic ice cap following the reduction of Russian SSBNs in the area.[58] However, these citizens have not remembered the salient point--if a country claims sovereignty over a piece of sea or land, they must have the means to enforce it. These same Canadians also point out that the new Victorias cannot operate under the ice. They are afraid even a minimal under-ice capability would need a massive refit with AIP which would double the cost of the acquisition. This is not the case. The navy also maintains that they do not and will not maintain submarines solely for operating in the Arctic.

There is a perception in Canada that the navy wants submarines so it can stay in the big leagues with the Brits and Americans. Four diesel/electric submarines are not anywhere close to "the big leagues," in numbers or capability. They are a modest investment for a fiscally constrained nation who has to exercise sovereignty over immense ocean areas in an unstable world. They are the consummate vessel for navies of medium powers, a fact demonstrated by forty-four countries that operate conventionally powered submarines, including, by way of example, South Africa, Syria, and Venezuela.

Overwhelming expense is another much-touted argument against submarines. While it might be a defence against submarines built onshore and of the nuclear-powered variety, diesel/electric boats are much cheaper. They cost substantially less than frigates and are more versatile and less vulnerable. One submarine can monitor an area four times the size that a frigate can, and as we shall soon see, the Victorias/Upholders cost Canada no new money to acquire.

In 1994 dollars, the navy calculated the daily operating costs of the naval assets we operate against those of the new Victorias. The figures in Table 2 show just how reasonable submarines are to operate, and given their unique characteristics and versatility, are probably the first vessels any navy should acquire. Canadians also need to realize that if we disband our submarine service, the navy will have to buy more ships and aircraft to make up for the loss, as well as using old equipment that is costly to keep running. So the cost savings abolitionists promote are unlikely to materialize.

Much erroneous information about the cost of the British Upholders has circulated around the country[59]; it has even penetrated the community of retired submariners. Canadians have been told that the price tag of $800 million is just the start--the expensive modifications, training, upgrades, and shore facilities are going to be extra. One group even added the cost of refits and operations into the acquisition costs to pad the final figure. The announcement in 1998 states that the contract *includes* these extras, excluding operating costs, for a total of $750 million offset over eight years, which represents about one quarter of normal acquisition costs. The Department of National Defence will recover much of the cost by paying off old destroyers and granting Britain training rights at Canadian bases at no charge. Always kept separate, the cost of operating and maintaining the four new boats is about the same as it was for the three old O boats.

> Motherhood issues like the following get the most press:
> *"Government cancels national day-care program and keeps submarines."*
> *"No submarines before a cure for breast cancer."*
> *"Health care in crisis and navy gets more ships."*

The media like to sell newspapers and get us to watch newscasts with headlines such as these. They capture our attention, inflame our emotions, and appeal to our sense of justice. They also send a message that is incorrect. These headlines lead Canadians to believe that money is taken out of our social welfare budgets to improve the Canadian Forces. This has never happened in the history of Canada and probably never will. Defence and social programs are not an either/or issue. Neither is defence spending an alternative to social spending, it is a complement. Canadians are entitled to *both* protection and a good social safety net. Social programs are a requirement but they do not remove the need to maintain a Canadian presence on the fishing grounds or elsewhere on our sovereign seas; nor do they mean we will cease assisting the oppressed abroad. Defence ensures our international trade prospers, which directly influences the size of our social spending and the availability of reasonably priced merchandise from around the world. Furthermore, defence spending is an insurance policy that helps us provide the security within which we enjoy pensions, health care, and education.

A well-known Canadian historian, Professor John Granatstein, speaking to the Special Joint Committee on Defence remarked, "The country must not stint at purchasing equipment. In good conscience, we cannot and should not send our forces into hazardous situations where their equipment is unmatched. Those service men and women are our sons and daughters. If we are to order them to keep the peace or to fight in Canada's interest, they need the best available equipment."[60]

The last word should go to the majority of Canadians. They have made it clear that they want to protect Canadian sovereignty including the capability to monitor, control and deter attacks on Canadian territory, waters, and airspace, as well as assist where required in maintaining domestic and international peace and security. They deemed submarines were necessary to achieve all that.[61]

Summing up the arguments in favour: submarines' independent mission flexibility varies from an unprovocative surveillance posture to specific operations against illegal fishing, drug and migrant smuggling and terrorists, through to a full warfare capability. The submarine sends a clear signal to potential adversaries that Canada is prepared to exercise its authority.

There is no middle ground in the debate for and against the acquisition of submarines for Canada--we either get them or get out of the business. There is no substitute.

Chapter 11
CANADA'S RECORD IN
SUBMARINE ACQUISITION

The official attitude of the country towards submarines is best exemplified by Canada's record in submarine acquisition. It is dismal--always procrastinating; always going for the cheapest option; always getting too few; always uncertain, always unprepared. It is small wonder that other nations who try to sell submarines to Canada are wary--our governments have dithered or changed their minds just once too often.

The first hasty purchase in 1914 of *CC1* and *CC2* was really an accident because British Columbia's premier would have preferred a dreadnought, but all he could find at *le moment critique* were two small submarines. The second two boats, *CH14* and *CH15*, donated by Britain in 1919 were not wanted by the RCN at all, despite an articulated requirement. Once more unprepared for war, the Canadian navy had to beg Britain for training submarines from 1940 onwards, and after they had learned the lesson the hard way, took ten years to convince the politicians that submarines were a necessity for Canada. It resulted in a borrowed British squadron in the 1950s. When Britain made it clear they expected

Canada to become more independent regarding submarines and the pressure to provide more submarine training days for the fleet increased, *Grilse* was rented from the USN in 1961. In the 1960s, the RCN made an unsuccessful bid for nuclear-powered boats. When the three Oberon class boats arrived in Halifax in the late-1960s it was the first serious acknowledgement by a government that Canada needed our own submarines. But the second batch of three, destined for the west coast, was not pursued by Pierre Trudeau's Liberal government and Canada was left with too few and no capability in the Pacific from the mid-70s on.

The current acquisition program to replace the three old Os has been no different. On and off again for nearly fifteen years, delayed by another unsuccessful attempt to acquire SSNs again in 1987 by the Tory government of Brian Mulroney and stymied by the lack of resolve of the Liberal government of Jean Chretien, it has followed Canada's historical pattern. Our submariners despaired, the navy's frustration escalated, and the population voiced little opinion.

Desperation, opportunism, and creativity drove the purchase of Canada's first submarines, not planning. The whole process took days, not years. A week before WWI was declared, a group of concerned citizens in Victoria, British Columbia, met to discuss the troubling state of the Pacific coast defences, which had been grossly neglected. They also heard from an American, who had joined them for lunch, about two submarines his Seattle shipyard had built and the Chilean navy had rejected.

As the world tensions escalated, naval headquarters in Ottawa cabled the dockyard at Esquimalt saying, "Guard against surprise attack." The navy showed this warning, which referred to two German cruisers in the Pacific that were heading up the coast of North America, to the premier of BC, Sir Richard McBride. McBride, believing that Victoria and Vancouver were about to be shelled and having been informed of the availability of the submarines in Seattle, hastily bought *CC1* and *CC2* before he received federal authority. He had them spirited out of Seattle under cover of darkness on 4 August 1914, just after Canada learned that we were at war. Canada took ownership of the new submarines a few days after they came alongside in Esquimalt.

Buying them at the drop of a hat was one thing, but manning them was quite another--the RCN had no submariners.

The records show that the precipitate decision by McBride was well intentioned, but he really had no idea if the boats were suitable, priced right, or if the navy could man or maintain them. Although it looked as if McBride presented the federal government with a *fait accompli*, the submarine acquisition was not. The premier and the senior naval officer on the west coast had asked permission to purchase the boats from the beginning but the naval service had been slow to respond. Their approval message arrived just after British Columbia received the boats.

McBride had done something no provincial premier would do today, or indeed would even be capable of doing: "His confidence was rooted in a surprisingly deep knowledge of Imperial defence, the naval history of the British Empire and Canada, and the current naval requirements of the Pacific coast."[62] He knew of the recommendation, made by the Admiralty two years before, that submarines were necessary for the RCN. However, McBride's actions certainly circumvented any indecision regarding the boats that he suspected would emanate from the Naval Service and the Conservative government of Sir Robert Borden.

Bad timing plagued the navy's addition of two H class submarines after the Great War, another unplanned acquisition. On several occasions, the RCN made it very clear to the Canadian prime minister that Britain's gift of *H14* and *H15* was kind but not wanted. In February 1919, when the navy was downsizing dramatically, had little operating money, and the crews of *CC1* and *CC2* had mostly returned to civilian life, Borden accepted the submarines. *CH14* and *CH15* served briefly, for twelve months in 1921/22, were soon de-commissioned and later scrapped. The tiny glimmer of hope which the British gift had given the preservation of the fledgling Canadian Submarine Service was extinguished.

The Canadian navy had little choice but to abandon the infant submarine branch; barely surviving between the wars as it was. The government wanted nothing to do with defence preparedness after "the war to end all wars" and very nearly starved the navy into extinction. But even if the RCN would have had the money and the manpower, it is extremely doubtful it would have had the vision to maintain *CH14* and *CH15* as target submarines to train their surface forces.

This shortsighted position led to the Canadian navy having no submarines at the start of WWII, a deficiency they failed to resolve despite several opportunities throughout the hostilities. The decision-makers in the inter-war RCN had limited insight regarding submarines, were already demonstrating their partiality for surface vessels, and still held a core belief that Britain would provide for her former colony if the worst came to the worst. This reliance on others turned out to be a mistake, costly between the wars and very costly indeed during the Second World War.

When the navy realized that they would have to train thousands of sailors and hundreds of escort vessels in anti-submarine warfare techniques to combat the voracious U-boats, Canada asked Britain to supply the submarines necessary to do it. Of course, Britain had almost nothing to contribute, stretched as she was in the early years. The Admiralty did manage to pry loose a few vintage submarines from their reserve fleet and a few antique American boats they had acquired in the lend-lease agreement. Later, after the tide turned in the Allies favour, some U-class submarines arrived in Canadian waters too. There were never enough and the convoy task groups suffered accordingly. At the end of the war, the navy was still sending escorts to sea that had not exercised with a live submarine or with the other ships in their task group.

Amazingly, there were at least two opportunities for Canada to divert a shipyard from building corvettes to constructing submarines. However, archival documents show that the senior naval officers were fixated on procuring surface vessels and let the chances slip through their fingers. Some tried to lay the blame on the Admiralty for the fiasco, but in truth, it was the head of the RCN and the Naval Board's fault that we did not have submarines for training in WWII. Right to the end, these senior officers persisted in their belief that Canada should not operate submarines and that Britain would provide enough, despite all evidence to the contrary. The operational commanders at sea could scarcely believe it and delivered increasingly loud and numerous pleas to headquarters, to no avail.

With a change in naval leadership in early 1945, a more independent vision blew through headquarters, sweeping away some of the traditional reliance on the Royal Navy. Some senior officers recognized the lesson that WWII had taught the RCN and they were determined to have submarines in the projected peacetime fleet. Their next battle, waged in the political arena, was to set a pattern of government reluctance that was difficult to overcome, and would continue for years.

The RCN included five U-class submarines in their post-war plans but documents demonstrate that Cabinet refused to consider their grandiose vision and preferred the idea of a small coastal defence navy without submarines. Strangely enough, it was not the navy's continued requests, but the politicians' yearning to increase Canada's voice abroad through the newly formed NATO that set the RCN on the path to restoring our submarine service. The government soon realized Canada needed to contribute a vital element of defence to collective security arrangements to achieve any influence with their allies and this resulted in the navy specializing in ASW. And an ASW navy has to have training submarines.

Even with all that, Canada still did not acquire her own boats for another sixteen years. Initially, the RCN tried to rely on borrowed submarines, again with dismal results. Instead of providing a year-round boat, the RN offered one submarine for two months--hardly what the RCN had anticipated. Their request to the US fared no better. After those eye openers in the late '40s, the RCN began to include the rental of a full-time submarine in their budgets. However this scheme also proved unsatisfactory and did nothing to promote self-reliance.

The early 1950s heralded escalation in requests for the use of training submarines in the RCN, which made impossible demands on a single boat. The projection for 1952-53 showed that three submarines were needed to provide the 725 submarine training days on the east coast and 240 on the west. The RCAF was also in on the act, requiring submarines with which to train their aircrews on an increasing basis. Clearly the rental option was not cutting the mustard, though the politicians preferred it to the thought of having our own submarines. The reasons for their reluctance in developing a Canadian Submarine Service are not very clear in the records and were probably related to a perception that submarines were nasty, ungentlemanly vessels that did nothing but sink ships. This was not what they wanted to be seen supporting.

The first recommendation to establish a submarine service reached the Cabinet defence committee in 1954 and failed to win approval. The politicians demanded that the RCN continue to rent training boats despite clear evidence to the contrary. However the navy had little choice but abandon the plan for its own submarine component and soon the idea to rent a whole squadron emerged. The Royal Navy's Sixth Submarine Squadron (SM6) arrived in Halifax in 1955 and stayed for eleven years, supplying three boats for the east coast, but never any for the Pacific. Although SM6 delayed the establishment of our own submarine service, it did stalwart service for the Canadian ASW fleet and aircraft. At the same time 200 Canadians trained and served in British submarines as the *quid pro quo*. These men were to become the first Canadian submariners of the modern era and, although not planned, later enabled Canada to man her own boats in the 1960s.

In the late 1950s the RCN reactivated their proposal to the government for a submarine branch, recommending that Canada build seven or eight boats. They timed its presentation to the politicians to coincide with a Conservative government assuming power in 1957. Forced into a decision by the Admiralty announcing they could no longer guarantee three boats for SM6 and that Canada had to man the squadron themselves, the new minister of national defence started to consider re-establishing the Canadian Submarine Service. The clincher came in 1958 when the USN offered Canada a boat from their reserve fleet for the cost of reactivation only. The RCN recognized that acceptance of this offer was only an interim solution to the lack of ASW training boats but knew it would tide them over while they were planning to build their own. Cabinet approved the plan on 8 January 1960 and HMCS *Grilse* arrived in Esquimalt eighteen months later, resurrecting our submarine service after nearly forty years. It had taken fifteen years to persuade the politicians but at least this time round the establishment of the submarine service and *Grilse's* acquisition had been deliberately planned. The Tories began to publicly articulate their desire to build submarines in Canada.

At the same time as all this was happening, the seminal event in submarine development took place. The world's first nuclear-powered submarine, USS *Nautilus*, was launched in 1954 providing independence from air, sustained high underwater speed, and almost complete invisibility. In late 1957 the Canadian government asked the navy to choose which types of vessels they wanted to have nuclear power. Within a month the RCN implemented a study into nuclear-powered submarines and a month after that they signed the first of several agreements with the US to exchange marine reactor information. The naval officers involved with the study soon determined that SSNs were a better, cheaper, and less vulnerable ASW platform than surface ships--a heretical opinion in a navy that had never espoused the operational role of submarines. Even so, the Chief of Naval Staff, Vice Admiral H. G. DeWolf, RCN, DSO, DSC, embraced the idea and confidently announced in 1958, "Nuclear submarines will... make up half of Canada's fleet."[63]

After the initial enthusiasm waned and DeWolf's retirement, the navy's resolve faltered. They were stumbling over the huge expense involved and were concerned enough to take the figures to the Cabinet defence committee three times in six months for reassurance to continue the SSN study. The navy's first proposal resulting from the study, exemplifying their anxiety, offered the government two options--twelve nukes or twelve diesel/electric boats. Approved in principle, the government deferred the choice on the type of submarine until they had more details. Three months later the RCN's second proposal leaned more towards diesel/electric submarines, suggesting the British Oberon class or the US Barbel class, and dropped the number to six or eight. The politicians again demanded more information, this time about the two classes of conventional boats. Eight months after they first asked the government to consider SSNs, the navy abandoned them completely and recommended that Canada build six Barbels. Because they were substantially more expensive than the Oberons, the RCN proposed that they do so at the expense of six planned surface ships. The government of the day remained unhappy--they demanded that the navy get permission from NATO to replace some of the NATO-tagged surface ships with submarines. The next permutation had the navy asking for six Barbels, which they felt would benefit NATO, or six Oberons (in two batches of three) and four ASW frigates that would benefit Canada *and* NATO. Amazingly, once the permission had arrived from NATO to exchange ships for submarines, the RCN did not use it as a lever to get the politicians to decide--they were sure that soon the Barbels would be theirs.

Unfortunately the RCN had not factored in Diefenbaker's dislike of President Kennedy, or his tendency to procrastinate. The Americans withdrew their Barbel offer in August 1961 in retaliation for Dief's behaviour over the US Bomarc missiles and the navy quickly reverted to a training submarine mentality and the British Oberons. In March 1962, the Cabinet approved three Oberons from Britain (a reduction of three) and eight frigates to be built in Canada (an increase of four). From twelve SSNs to three diesel/electric boats was quite a sea change.

In approving the British submarines the Cabinet did not rule out the prospect of Canada acquiring nuclear-powered boats in the future. This led to another RCN study fuelled by the navy's disappointment in losing the Barbel submarines and their uncertainty over whether their submarine requirement was for operations or training. The 1962 Submarine Committee report, which found an operational need and again recommended twelve SSNs to counter the Cold War submarine threat in all areas of Canadian maritime responsibility, never reached the Naval Board, let alone Cabinet.

Although the Canadian Submarine Service was reborn as a result of this tortuous process, the result was inadequate and Canada has lived with it for thirty-five years. Some of the blame can be laid at the government's door--the politicians were paralyzed by the expense of SSNs and were offended by the idea of operational submarines. (In the early 1960s, nuclear power was not the emotional issue it is today.) However the navy did not manage the acquisition well either--throughout they failed to present a firm, united front or a clear idea of why they needed submarines. In the end the RCN's need to have anything that operated underwater weakened their resolve to hold out for SSNs or the Barbels. Their ultimate choice had the Canadian Submarine Service destined to operate too few submarines of two different nationalities--a logistical and personnel nightmare that was to haunt the service for a decade.

It was not smooth sailing from here either. The Conservative government postponed the purchase in September 1962 and then lost the general election in 1964. Paul Hellyer became the new Liberal minister of national defence and ordered a review of all procurement programs. While it waited, the RCN kept pressing the government for a conclusion on the submarine deal with Britain and decided they must acquire more US boats to solve the short-term need of 2000 submarine training days/year. When Hellyer cancelled the frigate program, tied as it was to the new boats, in October 1963, the RCN despaired. But he did not scuttle the three Oberons; Cabinet approved the purchase in November after Hellyer negotiated a $33 million deal with his British counterpart. The proposed second batch of three was not mentioned, and was never heard of again.

SM6 continued to operate out of Halifax under a new contract which was distinctly disadvantageous to Canada, and *Grilse* operated from Esquimalt to alleviate the acute lack of training submarines during the construction of the Oberons. In 1968, HMCS *Rainbow* from the USN joined *Grilse* on the west coast as the last O boat was delivered. Presumably, the delay in the planned procurement of used US submarines occurred because the RCN was reluctant to approach the government for more submarines when they were having such difficulty with the Oberon/Barbel acquisition.

When the last boat of SM6 returned to the RN, Canada had five submarines of her own--two of American descent on the west coast and three, considered second-best, from Britain on the east coast. But *Grilse* did not sail again, so we went down to four. At the end of 1974, *Rainbow* was de-commissioned and since that time there has been no submarine in the Pacific fleet. HMCS *Ojibwa, Onondaga,* and *Okanagan* have operated out of Halifax, with only two brief visits to Esquimalt in thirty years.

Augmentation of the submarine squadron remained a priority for the navy through the 1970's. It tried for another O boat for the west coast at the time of *Okanagan's* commissioning and again when *Rainbow* went to the breakers, both attempts proving unsuccessful. The navy came very close in 1978 when Britain offered a new-to-you O boat and Treasury Board approved the funds. However, the Chief of Defence Staff decided to put the money towards a future submarine replacement program, little knowing that it would be twenty-two years before that dream became reality. Though unsuccessful, these efforts resulted in one important gain--those who had carried the flame through the late 1970s and early '80s managed to get a proposal to acquire ten to twelve submarines incorporated into the Canadian Forces long term plan. If they had not persisted and received some support, the navy likely would not have considered replacement submarines at all.

The first real planning to replace the Oberons came in the very early 1980s. One of the submariners who initiated the push for recognition of the submarine need decided to take the proposal to Cabinet. The navy did little to encourage his intentions and it took until 1983 to make the program official--CASAP, the Canadian Submarine Acquisition Program, was inaugurated in May. CASAP planned to build new boats onshore and only considered diesel/electric submarines with the potential for under-ice capability. With the program well underway and ready to go to tender at the end of 1986, there was an unexplained delay. In June 1987 the Tory government of Brian Mulroney presented their new defence policy which contained a plan for twelve nuclear-powered submarines. The sudden switch stunned the submarine community and irritated the hopeful diesel/electric builders around the world.

It was almost exactly twenty-five years since the last skirmish with nuclear-powered submarines but this time there seemed some hope of success because the government itself had originated the idea. The navy, knowing a good thing when they saw one, drove ahead with almost indecent speed and fell all over itself to make the new program stick. Of course it didn't, as many astute observers predicted, and this mightily annoyed the SSN contenders, France and Britain, who had spent millions pursuing the huge contract.

Myriad reasons brought the SSN acquisition down. The Cold War ended; the feasibility study was done in haste with insufficient data; the program was improperly constituted which brought the navy into conflict with the Treasury Board; the costing was flawed; and some of the procurement decisions were questionable.[64] At the same time the government had to make a decision for or against SSNs, there was the added pressure of another factor peculiar to latter-day politics--optics. How could the Tories cancel their promised national day-care program in the 1989 budget and continue with SSNs? So finally, it was the opinion of the sales strategy group of the 1989 budget that tipped the balance away from the submarines. And not as many thought, the opposition of the peace lobby.

After the April 1989 federal budget, the navy had no submarine replacement program at all, the original diesel/electric acquisition having been cancelled soon after the SSNs were announced. The navy was left with neither a prospect of new boats nor much credibility with the politicians.

Regrouping took time--the Berlin Wall fell, a new world order evolved and Canada's security needs changed to meet it, a new Liberal government came to power in 1994, and our national debt soared. Submarines suddenly did not seem so essential anymore and defence fell right off the government's agenda except as the object of sweeping cuts. What concerned the navy in the early 1990s was that the Canadian Submarine Service was in serious danger of disappearing through neglect unless something was done to rescue it. The Oberons were approaching thirty years old--geriatric in submarine terms--and the navy was not going to be able to operate them safely much longer, even though the navy's missions required them.

The replacement submarines proved almost impossible to restore to the defence department's wish list in the 1990s. The navy renamed the emasculated acquisition the Canadian Patrol Submarine Program, gave it a few staff, and absorbed it back into their departments in headquarters. The new program went from six to eight diesel/electric boats in the early 1990s and down to four in 1994 while weathering several deferrals. The Liberal defence review of 1994 was the program's last chance. The Special Joint Committee on Defence stated that although there was a concrete case for submarines for Canada, the cost of replacing the ageing O boats with new submarines costing about $3 billion was prohibitive. They inferred that unless a bargain could be found and no new money need be spent, the proposal should be abandoned.

But the bargain had already been found. In 1993, Britain, with their traditional flair for timing, had offered four slightly used Upholder class submarines to Canada. The British offer turned out to be the saviour for which the navy and the submariners had been praying, but it took five more years to materialize. The Liberal White Paper on Defence, announced in December 1994, hedged the government's bets but did disclose that they intended to explore the Upholder option further. However, the policy statement failed to inspire much confidence in our submariners because the government did not say categorically they would preserve the Canadian Submarine Service.

Any optimism the navy had dissolved again when the Liberals dropped the Upholders to the bottom of the defence department's shopping list in 1995. Britain, irritated at the message this sent, ended Canada's exclusive right to first refusal. When they offered the boats to Chile, Portugal, and South Africa, the Canadian submariners were greatly alarmed. The Upholder project got to Cabinet in the spring of 1996 and was approved by the ministers but stalled on the PM's desk--it seemed he alone had the power to preserve or kill our submarine service. Defence Minister Collenette announced that DND was not ready to proceed. Little more was heard for a year and the navy improved the proposal. They presented it to the new minister, Art Eggleton, saying, "Net cost of the acquisition has been reduced, additional offsets have been identified, and a stronger package of opportunities for Canadian industry is now included."[65] The briefing note also stated that the US would "compensate Canada for the opportunity for US forces to train with the Canadian diesel submarines."[66] Eggleton went to see the Upholders for himself in June 1997 and then word came that he had told the British sales team that he would announce a decision on the Upholders no later than 31 December 1997. Hope surged when the British PM, Tony Blair, discussed the submarines with Jean Chretien in October. But the December date came and went with no word.

Finally, when many outside the navy had given up, the minister of national defence announced on 6 April 1998 that Canada was acquiring the four Upholders for a song. In Halifax, Eggleton said, "These submarines are a great purchase for Canada, giving our navy a vital capability at a fraction of what it would otherwise cost and it will not require new money from our current defence budget."[67] The announcement of the replacement program caused a one-day flurry of activity in the press and was dead news after that.

The two submarine acquisition programs which have taken place since the late 1950s have been remarkably similar. Both took more than a decade; both were interspersed with a run at nuclear-powered boats; both resulted in submarines that were not the navy's first choice; both acquired British boats; both ended up with too few submarines; and both pitted the navy against the governments of the day. The theme that runs through Canadian submarine acquisition programs, indeed through most major defence procurement programs, is the politicians' unwillingness to make a decision. These delays have resulted in Canada's perennial unpreparedness. The political procrastination is caused by lack of understanding and vision, lack of resolve, lack of public support, and later, lack of money. In wartime it costs lives, and in peacetime it costs credibility.

Chapter 12
THE STRUGGLE FOR SUBMARINES

True support for submarines in the Canadian navy itself has been a recent phenomenon--growing out of the realization from all quarters that a navy must operate over, on, and under the sea to be effective.

Our navy has always had difficulty acquiring submarines. Even when our allies began to design their navies around submarines, Canada followed a more traditional line and ended up with an emphasis on the surface fleet and a submarine force that was too small and poorly utilized for years. The lack of support for submarines is very pervasive in this country--it has occurred in the past in the navy, in the political arena, amongst the citizens, and in the media. The difficulties in Canada's acceptance of submarines originate from perceptions, or more correctly misperceptions, which have persisted since *CC1* and *CC2* arrived in Esquimalt in 1914. The most fundamental influence that undermines submarine acquisition is Canada's inability to see itself as a maritime nation. Other beliefs include: peace-loving nations do not need a military; our NATO allies will provide what we don't have when we need it; our navy is a surface navy; and defence takes money from our social programs. All of these demonstrate a lack of defence tradition.

Our navy grew out of the British navy, was dependent upon it for years, and has operated within collective security arrangements throughout most of its short life. First it was a small arm of the huge Imperial navy and now it is an integral part of NATO and a contributor to UN and other multilateral security forces. Looking at naval matters independently has been difficult, not only for our navy, but also for our politicians. Old habits died hard and Canada believed for decades that if the RCN was short of a certain type of vessel our allies, generally Britain, would provide it, as exemplified by the requests for submarines post-WWII. When the Admiralty decided it was too expensive to continue providing assets to former colonies, the RCN still had an uphill battle with successive governments to get submarines of its own. Their inexperience in facing off with politicians led to several watered down submarine proposals and an Oberon acquisition that was considered, certainly by submariners, to be second best.

The Canadian navy also used to view itself as a surface navy, despite the anomaly of *CC1* and *CC2* in WWI. The well-known role of convoy protection in WWII not only defined our navy but also perpetuated this opinion, preventing several attempts to re-establish the submarine component from 1942-45. When the RCN adopted ASW as its post-war specialty, the government only acquired a token submarine force after pursuing rental boats for years, further reinforcing this outlook. This action was taken within the navy for two reasons. First, there were few, if any, submariners at the decision-making level in the navy then to promote the value of and the need for sufficient numbers of submarines; and second, the predominately surface officers saw little gain in supporting submarines. Furthermore, the surface fleet was in the majority and therefore had more clout when it came to operational and acquisition decisions. Conflict began to grow between the Canadian surface and submarine forces, certainly at the procurement level. The submariners saw themselves being treated as second-class citizens and the surface sailors saw the submariners as taking more of the declining defence dollar when their destroyers needed replacement.

The navy's identity crisis in the 1950s and '60s also had a hand in diluting support for Canadian submarines. Governments of that period had difficulty establishing the purpose and roles of the Canadian navy amid the growth of the Cold War, lack of money, and an almost remarkable reticence to make decisions. If the navy of the time had had clearer direction from its political masters, perhaps Canada would have established a more realistic submarine service then.

Another factor dilutes support for submarines, which is not restricted to the navy. Submarines make up a small percentage of Canada's warships and this has sent a silent message for thirty years to the navy, politicians, governments, and the public that they are not as important as frigates and other surface ships. Had Canada acquired eight to ten boats in the 1960s it is very doubtful many would view them as expendable now.

Governments as far back as 1914 have demonstrated singular indecisiveness when the navy has asked them to consider submarines. It is almost as if they believed if they decided to make no decision the issue would go away. Nor has it mattered much whether the governments were Liberal or Conservative. Liberals, on the surface, look the least likely to acquire submarines for Canada, but in fact, they have been the ones who signed the contracts for both the Oberons and the Upholders. The Tories, on the other hand, were the governments that seemed more interested in defence and backed both nuclear-powered submarine acquisitions. However, they failed to see them through.

Post-WWII politicization of defence procurement has been a serious obstacle to long-term naval policy development and planning. New governments coming into power tend to disassociate themselves from their predecessor's plans as fast as they can, sometimes cancelling them altogether, like the Liberals did with the EH-101 helicopters. Neither has the idea of a large, blue water navy gone over well with Canadian administrations, except during WWII. There has been a tradition of reducing the numbers of ships and submarines from 1910, when the RCN was established, right up to the present day.

Politicians have always targeted the defence department for spending cuts when times were hard and generally they have viewed our submarine service as expendable, partly because it is so small and partly because they do not understand its value. After all, submarines are not sent on as many trade missions or diplomatic visits as destroyers or frigates--they do not photograph well and do not provide comfortable locations for the social requirements of these events. The politicization of submarine acquisition has been disproportionately large in recent years because of the erroneous view that the boats are only good for sinking ships and that they fire nuclear missiles. The 1987, Tory initiative to buy twelve nuclear-powered submarines divided the country and the politicians into two opposing camps, each debating their side furiously, often without all the facts.

And the issue of optics has become increasingly important for governments as modern communications bring their actions right into the electors' living rooms for intimate dissection. Remember the negative press over the Liberals' helicopter flip-flop? Submarines are not vote getters--in fact, they are quite the opposite. It is a brave Canadian government who makes submarines a very public issue; generally, they prefer to keep their deliberations out of the public eye and the media, making submarine announcements at times when events that are more newsworthy are emerging to take up the copy space and airtime.

The fiscal predicament in which governments find themselves also has a negative affect on submarine acquisition. It either delays the process or prevents it. Couple lack of money with lack of resolve and there is a potent mix--it is easy to see why submarines have dropped to the bottom of governments' agendas over the years.

Political parties are sharply divided on defence. In Canada the Conservatives are viewed as the hawks and the NDP are the doves. Liberals often sit on the fence but Canadians, if asked, would tend to label them more as doves, despite the fact that they have spent more on defence than any other party--though this outcome is probably more by virtue of being in power longer than being pro-defence. It is fairly safe to say that most politicians see submarines solely as weapons of war. They have not taken it upon themselves to become informed, anymore than the Canadian public has, though arguably they should have.

Unlike Britain and the US, there is little defence constituency in the House of Commons. The members of Parliament who have served in the Canadian Forces can be counted on the fingers of one hand. The rest of the MPs in Ottawa have had little exposure to defence matters, even less about submarines. None of our recent ministers of national defence have been in the Canadian Forces or have had much, if any, connection with defence before taking office. Moreover, defence is not considered a plum job in Cabinet. In both the Mulroney and the Chretien Cabinets, there has been significant opposition to submarines. Joe Clark, as minister of external affairs and Michael Wilson, in finance, were against the nuclear-powered submarine acquisition in 1987 for different reasons, and Paul Martin, the present Liberal minister of finance, apparently disagreed with the Upholder acquisition. The finance portfolio carries much more influence than defence, being the senior Cabinet post and the one that holds the purse strings.

More recently, the country's preoccupation with the constitution and the possibility of the separation of Quebec has also had its effect on the current submarine replacement. Politicians could not seemingly grapple with more than one issue at a time and submarines, an unpopular topic at the best of times, were marginalized.

One naval writer made this telling, and all too accurate, comment about the Canadian persona: "One could call Canada a maritime state with a landlocked mentality."[68] The Special Joint Committee were more polite in describing the population's outlook on defence: "For Canadians who live far from the turmoil of tribal war and regional conflicts and who are not especially well-served by their news media, [defence] might seem like a low priority, and that accounts for much of the complacency we see today."[69] Canadians, fed inaccurate information by the media and unwilling to find out the truth for themselves, hold paradoxical opinions on defence, the navy, and submarines, as well as foreign policy issues. As we have seen before, polls demonstrate this when citizens are questioned about defence matters in general and about submarines in particular. The majority support first-rate armed forces but are unwilling to pay for them. Another interpretation of the 1997 poll on defence showed that 61% supported the Upholder submarine acquisition but did not want any money spent on the Canadian Submarine Service.

Robert Thomas, writing for the Canadian Institute for International Peace and Security, said: "The public see and know very little of its navy--only a miniscule part of the population routinely sees warships. Most operations and training take place far from public observation and are not inherently newsworthy. The importance of the sea and its resources are not widely understood and the current problems of the Atlantic fishery, for example, create an appearance of declining value to Canada. Government and public preoccupation with constitutional and economic matters is also significant."[70] As far as submarines go, few Canadians see them and few Canadians know a submariner. Both go about their business quietly and without fuss, preferring to maintain a low profile for security reasons.

The public image of the navy is still based on the Battle of the Atlantic in WWII because it was the RCN's Vimy--its coming of age. This view of a surface navy battling overwhelming odds, manned by young, unsung, weekend sailors has become embedded in the minds of the populace and is brought up every Remembrance Day. It is no longer valid, and along with the popular opinion that naval conflict ceased with the end of the Cold War, does a disservice to our present maritime forces that affects their ability to plan and operate. The public, seeing the navy asking for warships to use for fishery patrols, sovereignty purposes, and diplomacy, etc. in the 1990s, cannot resolve the difference between their outdated image of the navy and today's realities and thus withholds its support.[71] Submarines do not feature in the navy's popular image at all and suffer for it accordingly. Indeed, most Canadians do not even know that Canada has operated submarines, off and on, since 1914.

Furthermore, few organizations in Canada set an example of support for submarines Canadians can follow. Governments since 1919 have sent messages that display ambivalence to submarines at best and downright opposition at worst. Canada's other mouthpiece, that has the attention of our citizens and moulds opinion, is the media--and through that mouthpiece, the peace lobby--and they generally come out against submarines, usually very loudly. If the navy mounts a public relations campaign to raise awareness and support for submarines, Canadians see the efforts as having a bias, which indeed they have, and therefore their PR carries little weight.

Defence has only a small place in the identity of Canada, certainly for the majority of Canadians. We see ourselves as a peaceful, compassionate, inexperienced country. True, we are young in comparison to many nations and our early reliance on Britain has made it difficult for us to develop a separate and independent defence identity. Canada struggled hard to gain release from the mother country but was successful years before the navy chose to untie the apron strings of the Royal Navy. The delayed development of a naval tradition in Canada has led Canadians to fail to include it in their national persona. The United States, in contrast, had to go it alone after their War of Independence and developed a strong defence identity and national pride in their armed forces. The average Canadian has little comparable pride in our navy and our submarine service.

Unwillingness to foot the bill for submarines has occurred not only in tight fiscal climates, but also in times of plenty. And it has not only been the governments that did not want to pay, sometimes it has been the navy. For example, the Chief of Defence Staff declined the opportunity to obtain an O boat for the west coast in 1978 despite the need in the Pacific and having received approval from Treasury Board for $11.25 million with which to purchase it. The Chief of Defence Staff chose to hold the money for a submarine replacement program which took another twenty years to succeed.

It is fairly typical in warship procurement for the government to divide the navy's requirements into batches. The original Oberon acquisition was for six boats in two batches of three and the Canadian Patrol Frigate program was originally planned for three batches as well. When money is short, subsequent batches often fall by the wayside. It is done, of course, to space out the expenditures but it also offers an irresistible 'out' to governments that wish to renege on a commitment without much publicity.

As the national debt began to climb, governments deferred more and more defence spending for capital projects. It became harder and harder for the defence department to get naval, or any, procurement plans onto the government's agenda. Equipment decayed, prices rose, and available funds evaporated. Submarines were bumped so often that some believed it was the government's intention to let the service rust out and die a protracted death. The Upholder acquisition suffered at least three deferrals after the navy learned if they were serious about operating submarines, they had to develop creative acquisition methods.

Public and political support for submarines waned as the desire for a peace dividend grew after the Berlin Wall collapsed and the Cold War ended. It was a popular misconception that the dividend would take the form of savings derived from scrapping warships and aircraft. Submarines suffered the fate of being viewed as redundant in the new world order.

However Canadians did get the dividend they believed they were owed, though in a less obvious way. From 1990 to 1994, 13.5% was cut from defence spending, totalling nearly $21 billion in savings from planned expenditures, and more cuts were to come. This is an astounding figure when Canada has been paying for new frigates, and coastal defence vessels, etc., during that same period. These expenditures were necessary just to keep the navy afloat, not to augment it. Neglect, before 1989, had been severe and had to be addressed.

Canadians have a reputation for compromise and an ability to make the best of things. Does this characteristic influence submarine acquisition? There is good evidence that it has in the past and probably still does today. Canada bought the Oberons, which many believed were second-best to the American Barbels, and put the navy in the awkward position of operating submarines of two different nations for a while. Neither the O boats nor the Barbels met the Canadian requirements satisfactorily and the Oberons were logistically more difficult to integrate into the fleet and to maintain because their spares had to come from across the Atlantic. In war, this could have been a big problem. But the submariners did their best with what they had been bought and learned to excel anyway.

Recently it has been the Upholders or nothing--not much of a choice, especially if the British submarines were not ideal. Also, there are only four of them, with no prospect of getting any more. Mostly governments who have based their decisions on price and availability have chosen the submarines that Canada has acquired since 1962. The navy, knowing the alternative to disagreeing with the purchases is the loss of the Canadian Submarine Service, has been forced to compromise.

Strong, loud, and often based on limited logic and distorted facts, the peace lobby in Canada gets a lot of ink. Project Ploughshares, one of the best-known groups, has been vociferous in its opposition to submarines in the Canadian Forces. They know how to get the media's ear, conduct excellent PR campaigns, always write letters to the editor, and know exactly how to hit the public's hot buttons. The peace groups are also very good at appearing at events concerning defence matters and consultative processes with submissions, speeches, and personnel. For example, Project Ploughshares made in-person submissions in eleven of the fourteen cities that the Special Joint Committee visited during their defence review in 1994. This was far above any other group.

In 1989 when the Tories axed the nuclear-powered submarine program, the peace lobby took the credit and many believed they deserved it. The facts, however, show this was incorrect, but no one attempted to rectify it.[72] It is an example of their power that the public did not question it, but rather assumed it to be the case.

If Canadians knew more about their submarines, perhaps they would give more support to their replacement. Canadians have had little to read about their naval history. Scholarly works analyzing the navy and defence politics are a relatively recent arrival on our literary scene, starting to appear in the early 1980s. Before that, most books about the navy were anecdotal, personal memoirs, and written for propaganda purposes. Submarines were scarcely given more than a paragraph at best, a phrase at worst, until the mid-90s when two books were published devoted entirely to our submarine service. Prior to that, Canadians have had nowhere to learn about the achievements, struggles, and traditions of our submariners. The National Film Board of Canada serves Canadians poorly too--it reflects the arts and media focus that has been and is predominately anti-war and anti-military. It has not helped the submarines' recognition quotient.

Canadian opinion is greatly influenced by the media. Indeed some observers feel that the media creates the country's opinion--a very worrisome thought considering it is often sensationalism that sells news. Even so, the media's influence on government policy has never been greater. Instantly televised pictures and reports force governments to respond to a greater range of situations that do not directly affect the security of the nation but are of concern to its citizens. The UN efforts in Somalia in 1992-3 and in East Timor in 1999 are examples of how the public's concern for a humanitarian crisis can result in an extra military tasking.

Having said that, the majority of Canada's media coverage is domestic in emphasis, and rarely stretches far across the oceans of the world. Most of our daily papers focus on local events, with provincial news getting the lion's share of the pages after advertisements. Thus Canadians see, through the media's eyes, a view that is parochial rather than an international one that shows how Canada fits into the world scene. With this predominately close-to-home reporting, defence becomes less understood and consequently less of a priority to a nation looking primarily at its own belly button.

It is easy to see that if the press takes it into its head to ignore defence issues and the Canadian Forces, the public awareness diminishes and the importance of Canada's maritime character disappears for months on end. If the media does report on Canadian defence these days, it often leaves a negative impression, that try as the Department of National Defence might, cannot be easily turned around, events in Somalia notwithstanding. Despite all this, the navy realizes the most effective route to the Canadian public is through the media. They know if they give the press the correct facts, reporters are meant to give balanced accounts, but they also know it does not always work out that way. It is the peace lobby who so often up-stages the navy, getting their views to journalists first. Submarines, surrounded by out-of-date beliefs and emotional baggage, fare even less well at the press's hands than the surface fleet.

Hadley, in his chapter in *A National Navy*, shows that our navy's image is determined not only by what the navy is designed to do and what it can actually accomplish, but by what the public and the media feel the navy ought to be doing. For example, "...who needs warships for missions of peace"[73] is a commonly used reason for criticizing Maritime Command today, which in its turn, adversely influences public opinion on submarines.

In February 1996, the *Globe and Mail*[74] told Canadians that our military would be more likely to be engaged in support of international operations seeking global stability than anything else. It also argued that international peacekeeping needs only ground troops despite the fact that the Canadian navy has been involved in all recent coalition operations and is usually the first element of our armed forces that the government sends abroad. The *Globe* went on to say that Canada does not need a military force to defend itself, as there is no foreseeable threat. One wonders how they can be so sure that another threat will not emerge next month, next year, in twenty years... The editor also suggested Canada could no longer afford submarines, but failed to discuss the innovative funding mechanism the navy had released earlier. There was no explanation of how sovereignty works, how global stability enhances Canadians lives, or how the navy performs in relation to these key factors. It is precisely this type of editorial that gives Canadian citizens the wrong impression and moulds their opinions.

That same month the *Ottawa Citizen* told its readers Canada's navy had "entirely failed to justify the purchase"[75] of new submarines, by arguing that Department of National Defence had substantially reduced ASW and therefore did not need them. Informed Canadians know differently--surveillance skills and ASW skills are one and the same and cannot be maintained properly without submarines.

In August that year the *Vancouver Sun* wrote: "The British Upholder class submarine is an impressive piece of equipment, and four of the ever-so-slightly used subs for $1 billion is a good deal-- but it's a deal we can't afford and don't need."[76] More of the same. Nowhere in the popular press was there a positive opinion. Only in little-known periodicals were there pieces supporting the proposal.

When the Department of National Defence finally announced the Upholder acquisition, the media had not changed their tune. "Alas, we remain unconvinced that submarines *are* what is needed."[77] said the *Globe* the next morning. The editor also wrote that Canada needed better equipment for the army and more air transport capability instead. Five days before, another article in the same newspaper stated that Upholders are used principally "to detect and combat enemy subs."[78] Oh really?

With such reporting, it is no wonder the average Canadian does not believe Canada should have submarines in our fleet. The idea that public support for submarines is needed for development of political support may be true, but it will only happen when the Canadian media understand and report all the facts.

Useful support for the navy is lacking in Canada today in the public and political arena. This is caused by lack of knowledge and interest rather than lack of concern on the part of Canadians, by politicians placing popularity above the nation's best interests, and by negative press about the Canadian Forces--with little reported about the navy. Submarines suffer most from the country's lack of support. There is a sense that they have never been very important to Canada or we would have had more of them, as well as a perception that they are only good for sinking ships.

Unlike Britain, Holland, or France, Canada does not have maritime awareness entrenched in our national character. The navy is simply not a sufficiently strong part of our nation's fabric.

Chapter 13
SUBMARINES FOR THE 21ˢᵗ CENTURY

M uch has been written since the early 1960s about whether
we should have conventionally-powered or nuclear-
powered submarines, a debate which started in the early
'60s and continues today. However, a comparison of this kind can
be a bit like comparing apples and oranges--yes, they are both fruit
but they are completely different in character. SSKs and SSNs are
both submarines but they have vastly different propulsion systems
which provide characteristics suitable for performing different
tasks. Leaving cost out of the argument makes it easier to choose,
but is a facile exercise--expense can never be ignored. The navy's
concept of operations, our geography including the Arctic, the
distances involved, and the size of our maritime responsibilities
have some experts recommending nuclear-powered boats, but like
the majority of nations, the expense is just too much for us, to say
nothing of the public's unease with all things nuclear.

Now Canada has acquired new diesel/electric submarines,
and whether we like them or not, concerned Canadians need to
know if they are enough to meet Canada's requirements. Firstly,

conventionally powered boats are quiet, quieter than nukes, and this adds up to outstanding stealth, which is vital for surveillance as well as effective peacekeeping duties. Secondly, the power plants in the larger sizes are robust and efficient. Thirdly, conventional boats can have a distinct advantage in shallow, coastal areas whereas the larger, less manoeuvrable SSNs have done better in the open ocean operations of the Cold War, though this is changing. These shallow operational areas are the major focus of the underwater world since the end of the Cold War. For Canada's restricted coastal waters and big continental shelf it is also a plus. Fourthly, Britain and the US need conventional boats to train with, and NATO or the UN may need them for the multilateral operations we support. Fifthly, diesel/electric boats can still overcome huge odds and succeed--remember the Dutch submarine in the English Channel that "sank" five ships in an exercise. Sixthly, they are relatively simple when compared with the complexities of nuclear-powered boats and this keeps them relatively cheap. Diesel/electric submarines' acquisition and operational costs are easier to bear--navies can acquire between two to four conventionally powered submarines for the price of one SSN.

Modern diesel/electric submarines can be equipped with the same sensors and torpedoes as nuclear boats, so there is no advantage in those departments, and this alone makes their anti-surface warfare (ASuW) and anti-submarine warfare performance more than acceptable. Near total automation, which reduces crew size, is another benefit of current designs of conventional boats, saving personnel costs.

Undeniably, the sustained high speed the marine reactor gives SSNs and SSBNs underwater cannot be bettered in the submarine world. It improves their stealth and invulnerability by a huge amount, because they never have to snorkel to replenish their batteries and thereby risk detection. High speed can also be very useful once in a while to engage a contact or evade an attacker but it does come with a trade-off--increased noise. Nuclear power also gives submarines very long legs, which are especially useful when extended distances are involved domestically or there is a need to travel quickly to distant trouble spots.

And then there is the issue of the Arctic. So far, only nuclear-powered submarines which operate without the need for air can work under the ice. Diesel/electric boats do not have that ability, and for a northern country like Canada, it is a singular deficiency. If conventional submarines could be made to operate without snorkelling they could work in the Arctic and could gain some of the strategic and tactical advantages that SSNs also have elsewhere in the world's oceans. Fortunately, the technology to allow conventionally powered boats to do this already exists.

Air independent propulsion (AIP) or power, as the Canadian navy prefers to call it, is the technology that allows diesel/electric submarines to stay underwater for much longer periods without having to pay the premium for nuclear power and risk public censure. AIP has been dubbed the poor man's answer to nuclear propulsion. Work around the world has produced a variety of different methods including the Stirling engine, closed cycle diesel engines, closed cycle steam turbines, fuel cells, and small nuclear reactors. All these systems, except the small nuclear reactors because they do not produce the power of their big brothers, could in theory replace diesel/electric propulsion entirely. However studies have concentrated on hybrid systems that incorporate AIP with traditional diesel/electric plants, providing the power to maintain the charge in the batteries at low speeds. Most designs can be retrofitted to conventional submarines by cutting the boat in half and inserting a "plug" containing the system between the control room and the engine room.

An AIP system with an output of 300-400 kilowatts and an energy store of 100-megawatt hours is needed to power a 2000 tonne submarine at six knots for ten days without surfacing. It would use between 60-75 kW for propulsion and the rest for the "hotel load." The first full-size submarine that was modified and went to sea with an AIP system consisting of two Stirling engines was the Swedish *Nacken* in 1988. Such was the success after 6000 hours of operation that Kockums and the Royal Swedish Navy designed and built a boat with AIP incorporated from the beginning. This was the A19 Gotland class and the *Gotland* was launched in 1994. They now have four submarines each fitted with two Stirling engines at sea. The RSwN is reportedly pleased with the results, despite the high pressures and temperatures involved in the Stirling engine's operation. However, this system is limited in power output: about 75 kW per system which gives about two weeks of AIP at 5 knots. The Stirling engine is best suited for low speed surveillance operations, as it is quieter than a submarine running on diesels. Britain and Italy, among others, have been experimenting with closed or recycled diesel engine (CCD) systems and the Italians have one at sea in a mini-submarine. A benefit of the CCD is the ability to start on, or switch over to, outside air,thereby conserving stored oxygen and it can be built using off-the-shelf equipment. However, they come with several disadvantages--the most significant being that they are noisy. Chile has recently bought the French/Spanish joint-ventured Scorpene class AIP submarine with MESMA, the closed cycle steam turbine system which uses ethanol and oxygen for fuel and generates 4 kts. Pakistan's new Agosta 90B submarine will also have a MESMA system when launched in 2002.

Canada, being a northern nation, has been intensely interested in AIP for many years and our navy has a clear idea of what they want AIP to be able to do. Any system for serious consideration must include:

- increased submarine endurance (at least five times better);

- low acoustic signature;

- sufficient power output to provide a sustained submerged speed of 8 kts;

- high mean time between failures;

- low fuel consumption; and,

- simple, cost-effective, and reliable.

The navy's engineering branch believes it is fuel cells that are shaping up to be the most promising type of AIP. They are already used commercially in land applications, give the best range, and have the least drawbacks. Very simply put, fuel cells are devices that convert chemical energy into electrical energy by reverse electrolysis. The Canadian fuel cell from Ballard Power Systems of Vancouver consists of two electrodes separated by a proton exchange membrane (PEM) that is coated on each side with a thin layer of platinum catalyst.

A Ballard fuel cell.
(Credit: Ballard Power Systems)

Hydrogen and oxygen flow through channels in the anode and cathode, where electrons from the hydrogen are released and captured as electricity. The hydrogen protons combine with the oxygen to produce water vapour. (For more details, visit www.ballard.com)

The system requires relatively low fuel and simple storage requirements but produces a proportionately high-energy yield without combustion or any noise. In a submarine, oxygen would be carried as a cryogenic liquid and the hydrogen as a solid metal hydride or methanol, both stored externally to the pressure hull. The high cost and weight of a metal hydride might be a disadvantage but methanol is synthetic and renewable. Undoubtedly the fuel cells' high efficiency, low acoustic and thermal signatures, and safety offset any disadvantages. Fuel cell technology like Ballard's has the additional benefit of being environmentally friendly--the only by-products of the chemical reaction are potable water and heat at a very manageable 90 degrees Celsius.

While the German Siemens fuel cell, developed with Ballard proton exchange membrane (PEM) technology and using solid metal hydride as fuel, has been successfully trialled in the German submarine *U-1*, Ballard's Canadian version has not. The German navy intends to incorporate the technology in its next generation of diesel/electric submarines, the Type 212. However, the Canadian cell is undergoing further development with public funds in the hopes that it can be used in the new Victorias.

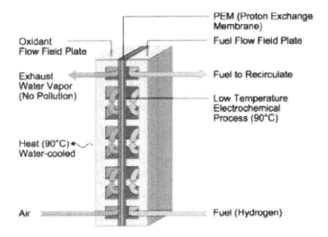

Diagram of a Ballard fuel cell showing how it works: each cell produces 0.6 volts of electricity and, when combined with others into a fuel stack, is able to provide sufficient power for its particular application.
(Credit: Ballard Power Systems)

The cost of AIP is not clear at the moment. In 1991, a naval engineer estimated that AIP would add about 20% to the cost of a new diesel/electric submarine. As a comparison, it cost $20 million to retrofit a Stirling engine into a submarine in 1991. How much a Ballard fuel cell plug would cost to put in our new Victorias is unknown but experts predict it will be affordable. Liquid oxygen as a fuel is readily available in Canada and its cost is similar to that of diesel fuel. No additional crew requirements are anticipated in an AIP submarine and personnel training will be done using a shore-based trainer. The Department of National Defence expects that fuel cell maintenance will be minimal at sea, as they have no moving parts and long operating lives.

Safety of AIP technologies provides an interesting study. The use of the hydrogen, liquid oxygen, hydrogen peroxide, etc. required by the various technologies is potentially hazardous, especially in a submarine, but with care and attention is not particularly dangerous. Ironically it is marine nuclear reactors that are by far the safest and most efficient form of AIP for submarines, although they are not usually considered to be in the AIP category.

The most viable AIP systems for Canadian submarines, other than nuclear power, appear to be the Stirling engine and the fuel cells. The noisiness of the closed cycle diesels is a major problem, unlikely to be overcome sufficiently, for it is just when a submarine needs to be silent that the AIP system will be in use. The Canadian naval engineers have also deemed the Stirling engine to be unacceptable due to the large plant size and low efficiency.

So it is to a home-grown technology that the Canadian navy is turning for its AIP system. Ballard Power Systems is a world leader in fuel cell production and the largest developer of proton exchange membrane (PEM) systems in the world. The Department of National Defence has been involved in the development of this technology since 1984, providing seed money and holding the rights to several key PEM patents.

With research and development funding from the Department of National Defence, Ballard completed a successful 50 kw fuel cell demonstrator in 1997 and is working towards a full-scale land-based model. This will produce an output of 400 kw, which would enable a submarine to remain submerged for three weeks while operating silently at low to moderate speeds. The investment to achieve this step in the development of a submarine fuel cell is estimated to be about $50 million over five years. More money will be needed to develop the air independent life support systems that go along with this technology and to design the integration of the systems into a Victoria. Hopes are high that the fuel cell plug will be ready by 2003. The Department of National Defence assesses the development risk as medium to low due to the major commercial investment already committed for its application in automobiles and buses, three of which operate every day in Coquitlam, British Columbia, for BC Transit.

This project, covered in maple leaves, is an exciting and potentially lucrative one for Ballard and Canada. It also means more Canadian jobs, always a strong selling point to politicians and the public. Experts are confident of the fuel cell's success and many countries who operate diesel/electric submarines are watching with mounting interest. The Department of National Defence is anticipating a substantial return on their investment over the next twenty years.

Ultimately the acquisition of submarines is subordinate to affordability. No nation should procure submarines at the expense of other equally important programs. Canadians have to ask, "Should we be replacing the O boats when our defence spending has been reduced? And, is it feasible for Canada to acquire submarines given our nation's debt at the turn of the century?" These are important questions--both philosophically and practically. Hopefully the philosophical one has been satisfactorily answered in previous chapters. The second question is perhaps better stated as, "Can Canada afford new submarines in 2000?" or "Is the return on the investment justifiable?" We should also look at the trade-offs, if any.

Money for submarines comes out of three different "pots" contained in the budget managed by the Department of National Defence--capital, personnel (P), and operations and maintenance (O & M). While DND's discretionary limit is high, any project over $100 million has to be approved by Cabinet.

Let's take one year's budget as an example and see what the navy and submarines use from it. In the fiscal year 1994-95 the navy cost Canada only 21% of the $11.5 billion defence budget. It used 11.25% of defence's P and O & M money and 44.3% of the available capital funds. While the POM expenditures do not vary much, the capital budget for the navy goes up and down in relation to the other two services depending on how much acquisition is going on--the high capital expenditure in 1994/95 reflected the tail end of the frigate program.

Submarine acquisition costs usually come out of the navy's capital budget, and while expensive, they are much less so than for frigates--60% less. Diesel/electric submarines cost between $300 and $750 million to build onshore or to purchase new offshore and off-the-shelf depending on their size and sophistication. Used submarines cost substantially less--the Victorias work out to about $152.5 million each, if we were paying cash for them, and two of the four are almost brand new. They cost Britain about $2.2 billion to build--that is $550 million each ten years ago.

To set submarine financial requirements into further perspective, the three Oberon class submarines used a little over $19 million, or about 0.6% of defence's entire O & M budget. The Victorias are expected to use less, although there is one more. Personnel costs add another $13.8 million per year that should remain relatively unchanged as the Victorias will use the same number of personnel. Another way of looking at the financial value of submarines is to compare them with our other naval assets: One frigate sea day = 2 hours of a maritime patrol aircraft = 10 submarine days. It costs $25,000 per day to operate a frigate and $5000 per day to operate a Victoria class submarine. Not only will the new submarines cost less to operate than our O boats did, they will yield an increase in potential sea time. This huge improvement in availability is derived mainly from lower maintenance needs.

Submarines yield more utility, more capability, and more flexibility for 66% less money than it costs to operate a frigate, and considering the capability they add to the fleet, they are a bargain to acquire and operate by anybody's reckoning.

Acquisition and operating costs of submarines are a small in comparison to Canada's $37 billion a year spending for employment insurance and pensions, and it must be remembered, the Victorias are not adding one cent to our deficit. The Liberal government of Jean Chretien made it very clear to the navy that if they wanted submarines they must be affordable within the defence budget. A tall order if some "new-to-you" submarines had not been found. The government's White Paper in 1994 said:

> *The Special Joint committee on Canada's Defence Policy found that submarines can conduct underwater and surface surveillance of large portions of Canada's maritime areas of responsibility, require relatively small crews, can be operated for roughly a third of the cost of a modern frigate, and work well with other elements of the Canadian Forces. It also recommended that, if it should prove possible in the current environment of military downsizing around the world to acquire three to six modern diesel/electric submarines on a basis that was demonstrably cost-effective (i.e., that could be managed within the existing capital budget), then the Government should seriously consider such an initiative. The United Kingdom is seeking to sell four* recently constructed *conventional submarines of the Upholder class, preferably to a NATO partner. The Government intends to explore this option.*[79]

With budgets dropping, the navy had to come up with some way of getting the Upholder acquisition to work within the government's demands, otherwise the Canadian Submarine Service would disappear, and quickly. Out came the pencils and thinking caps. The navy came up with an approach that did not increase the defence budget, did not take money out of the capital pot, did not sacrifice capability, and did not affect any other programs inside or outside the defence portfolio. (The details of how they did it are found in Chapter 14.)

Preparedness is a difficult concept for the average Canadian to grasp. The tangible part of the concept is made up of the ships, aircraft, and sailors but the navy is far removed from most of the population and conducts most of its business out of sight of land. The abstract part of the concept is of little interest to Canadians unless we are involved in a war. However, if we believe that Canada is worth protecting and that world peace is desirable, this country has to acknowledge that being reasonably prepared has its price. Canadians have to be prepared to be prepared. Many are not.

This attitude is not new--it was prevalent before both world wars and during the Cold War. It has cost Canada lives, lives of our sons and daughters, which could not be spared. The losses in the North Atlantic in merchant and naval vessels in WWII can in part be laid at the government's doorstep through its poor record in preparedness. Warships went to sea ill-equipped and ill-trained to combat the U-boats, right to the end of the war and their merchant cousins paid dearly for it. These are the consequences of being too prepared for peace.

Chapter 14
VICTORIAS AHOY!

Major naval procurement needs long lead times. Acquisition programs often begin a decade or two before the vessels are required, as the ships can take years to design, build, and trial before they join the fleet. Personnel training for new classes of vessels can also take several years and has to be woven into the planning and construction process. It is certainly easier to buy vessels off the shelf but they do not necessarily come with all the equipment the navy wants or are compatible with the rest of the Canadian fleet. But the financial premium that has to be paid to design and build our own boats has always been an obstacle for Canadian submarine acquisition programs. Although many jobs would be created if we built at home under licence as the Australians have done and we would gain submarine independence, the government has never seen the justification for such a choice.

The origins of the Oberon submarine replacement program can be traced to the early 1980s, when Jim Bell, a former submarine captain, working with Jim Wood, managed to get a proposal for ten to twelve boats onto the Canadian Forces long-term plan. The work did not gain official recognition in the Department of National Defence until 1983 when it was christened CASAP (the Canadian Submarine Acquisition Program). In 1984, the team moved into its own offices and began powering up to acquire eight diesel/electric submarines in two batches of four. On 11 October 1985 following Cabinet approval, the new Tory defence minister gave the go-ahead to acquire the first four boats. The Department of National Defence was close to choosing a diesel/electric design when Brian Mulroney's Tory government announced in 1987 that it would build twelve nuclear-powered submarines. This ambitious program sank two years later leaving the navy without fallback position, the earlier conventional program having been cancelled. The navy recovered slowly from its loss of credibility with political leaders over the highly criticized SSN procurement and finally achieved success with the British Upholder contract in 1998 after a nine-year struggle. This particular submarine replacement took much longer than it should have--hitting obstructions and going down a couple of blind alleys during the twenty-year effort.

After the demise of the twelve nuclear-powered submarines in the 1989 federal budget, the submarine replacement program suffered severely. The program lost its position on the Department of National Defence priority list, and when the Berlin Wall fell in late 1989 and other western nations cut defence spending ferociously in the early 1990s, the Canadian navy worried, quite justifiably, that Canada had missed the boat on submarines altogether.

A defence review, ordered by the Tory government in 1989, proved difficult to achieve because the rapidly changing world order made decisions difficult, but it eventually included a recommendation for six diesel/electric submarines, half the original requirement. These were to be acquired in two batches of three--but *only* if budgets permitted--and possibly would include air independent power later on. Furthermore, the review diluted the previous emphasis on Canada's three-ocean responsibility, Arctic sovereignty was demoted, and the old O-boats were to be kept on life support through a life-extension program.

In the early 1990s the busy Canadian submarine project office had closed, and the staff--with its unique knowledge of submarine acquisition requirements and design--had been absorbed back into various directorates in defence headquarters. The newly named Canadian Patrol Submarine Program (CPSP), slow to accelerate, surfaced from the doldrums in late 1991 with plans to present a revamped diesel/electric program to Cabinet early in 1992.

CPSP officials considered four proven conventional designs: the British Upholder, the Dutch Walrus, the German TR1700, and the Swedish Type 471--the latter chosen for the Australian navy's new Collins class. The navy hoped to have the first boat in the water in 2000, but in April 1992, the Tory government deferred the project for two more years--years the navy felt could not be spared.

Two years and another federal election later, the current Liberal government swept into power with a promise to cut defence spending still further--one promise they did keep. The submarine replacement program changed its name yet again to SCLE (Submarine Capability Life Extension), perhaps hoping to be third time lucky. The 1994 defence review established that the cost of replacing Canada's submarine fleet at $3 billion would be prohibitive--unless a bargain could be found.

The bargain had, of course, already presented itself. The 1994 White Paper on Defence announced officially that the government intended to explore the option of acquiring the four recently constructed British Upholder class submarines the Royal Navy had declared surplus. The navy busily worked on a way to get the submarines without costing the Canadian taxpayer any money and without needing any "new" defence money to Canadianize them. They succeeded, but despite the innovative approach, the Liberal government again dropped the replacement submarines to the bottom of the Department of National Defence's shopping list in July 1995 to enhance the position of the helicopters and armoured personnel carriers. Britain, irritated by Canada's procrastination, withdrew Canada's exclusive right to first refusal and put the Upholders on the open market.[80]

The navy's hopes revived when the Cabinet considered and approved the Upholder acquisition in the spring of 1996, but sank soon after when no announcement was forthcoming. The navy is neither visible nor well known in Ontario, the province which holds the Liberal powerbase in Canada, and the PM may have felt that a positive submarine decision would not benefit the party at that time. Art Eggleton, the new defence minister, visited HMS *Upholder, Unseen, Ursula,* and *Unicorn* at their builder's (GEC Marine, now BAE Systems) facility in northern England in June 1997 but left the sales team still wondering about their prospects of a sale to Canada.* On March 17, 1998, Eggleton announced that the submarine negotiations were nearly complete but it evoked no response from the Canadian media. Finally, on 6 April 1998, Eggleton officially told the country of the acquisition when he was visiting the navy in Halifax. Canada renamed the Upholders the Victoria class in 1999.

HMCS Victoria
(Credit: BAE Systems)

To set the historic deal into perspective it is worth recalling that the UK spent $2.28 billion building the four Upholders in 1991 dollars and the total *value* of the Canadian acquisition program is only $750 million--$610 for the submarines and $140 million for their reactivation--in 1998 dollars. The new Australian Collins class is a useful comparison--it is costing the RAN $787 million to build *each* submarine. The Upholders, though slightly used, are a quarter of the cost--a bargain by anyone's standard--buy one, get three free!

The contract includes not only the boats, but their complete reactivation and Canadianization, classroom and on-the-job training of 380 dockyard and sea-going personnel, logistic and technical management support for five years, full documentation, and initial spares. Also in the package is the combat control system integrator that will be shipped lock, stock and barrel to Halifax. It is in this multi-million dollar facility that the sensors and weapons integration is developed, tested, and set up before being implemented in the boats and it incorporates four command team trainers. These include a full size replica of the combat system (tactical systems maintainer trainer), a full size control room simulator on gimbals, a machinery control trainer, and a weapons handling and discharge trainer. Although Canada will not be using the fire control system or the torpedoes presently in the British Upholders, this shore facility will be invaluable for the conversion and training. Spares, often problematic in a discontinued class, should be less so because the Upholders were designed to use 65% of equipment which is common to all RN submarines and which will also be used in the newly ordered British Astute class nuclear-powered attack submarines.

In the sweetest and most innovative deal ever negotiated by the Department of National Defence, the former British Upholders may turn out to be a money making proposition for the navy. As Canadian government contracts do not allow payment of interest or deferral of payments, the navy came up with a creative plan to

---

*The author followed the MND's visit to GEC-Marine/BAE Systems within ten days and heard first hand the reactions of the Upholder Sales Team.

acquire the Upholders that would not cost the Canadian taxpayers much, if anything. The Brits, keen to "sell" to a sister nation, embraced the Canadian navy's challenge and worked hard to enhance the industrial benefits and submarine self-reliance for Canada. The deal is an eight-year lease-to-own package with the transfer of the title for £1.00 at the end of the lease period. The potentially complicated liability and control issues were resolved when Canada agreed to assume full liability during the eight year lease and Britain relinquished its right to recall the boats if the world situation were to deteriorate before Canada actually takes full ownership.

In a remarkable trade that avoids any undesirable fluctuations in the foreign exchange rate, the lease payments of $76.3 million/year are almost entirely offset by the British forces' use of the training facilities at CFBs Wainwright (Alberta), Suffield (Alberta), and Goose Bay (Newfoundland). The remaining acquisition "costs" are being recovered by paying off eight old ships, saving about $160 million, and by avoiding the last Oberon refit costing $84 million.

Other benefits, estimated at $350 million, have also been negotiated and some are written into the contract, although they cannot be subtracted from the "price." There are direct and indirect industrial benefits worth $150 million and 200 civilian jobs being maintained in Atlantic Canada for thirty more years, which perpetuates our submarine expertise. The new Industrial Participation Program allows Canadian companies special access to British defence contracts to the tune of $100 million and BAE Systems has invited Canadian companies to participate in the UK-based phase of the reactivation. And $100 million of the $140 million reactivation costs is being spent in Canada. While not written into the contract, the retention of the British training programs in Canada also ensures that local economies around the training bases are sustained.

However, it is the side deal with the United States Navy which could make this acquisition into a moneymaking proposition for our navy. The US has promised several millions of dollars each year in cash and kind for the use of the new Canadian Victorias for fleet training, as they have no diesel/electric boats of their own with which to practise.

All in all, it is a good deal, reminiscent of private industry. The former Commander of Maritime Command and submariner, Vice Admiral Peter Cairns observed, "If the CEO of a corporation were to do a deal like this he would need a wheelbarrow to take his stock options and bonus to the bank."[81] Indeed! Even so, the national impression persists that the navy is following a very old-fashioned route by acquiring submarines, when it is in fact looking to the future and has acted very responsibly throughout.

The Victorias require some changes to meet Canadian operational requirements. These include modifying the torpedo tubes to accept the American Mark 48 torpedoes, used in the Oberons since the mid-80s, installing a Canadian communications suite, and adapting the attachment for the Canadian towed array sonar (TAS). The decision to retain the relatively new fire control system from the Os and install it in the Victorias was based on cost-effectiveness--it is cheaper to move and integrate it into the new boats than to retrain everyone on the unfamiliar British system. Besides, Canadian submariners prefer it. The changes required to the torpedo tubes and for the Canadian TAS are minor. There is considerable training to be accomplished before the crews and the boats become operational; this started early in 1999, running parallel with the submarines' reactivation.

After the Upholder acquisition announcement in April 1998, the Department of National Defence lost no time in starting the change-over from the O-boats. HMCS *Ojibwa,* which was refitted and returned to service in May 1996, was paid off almost immediately in May 1998 to become the advanced harbour-training submarine for all ranks. HMCS *Okanagan*'s planned refit for the summer of 1998 was abruptly cancelled and she was decommissioned in September 1998 and was used for spares to keep *Onondaga* operational until July 2000, when she was paid off. HMCS *Olympus,* the non-operational basic harbour training boat, is retained in that role.

The Upholders will be coming to Canada out of order. Instead of arriving first, *Upholder* will be delivered last because she is the oldest and has more to be done. The first submarine to arrive will be *Victoria* (formerly *Unseen*) in late 2000, followed by *Windsor* (*Unicorn*), *Corner Brook* (*Ursula*), and *Chicoutimi* (*Upholder*) at six monthly intervals. BAE Systems is reactivating all four submarines in the UK with Canadians on-site. Our navy will accept the boats at the "safe to dive" stage after trials alongside and at sea. Once the boats get to Canada, they will complete a six-month work period alongside to install the fire control system from the Oberons, a new ESM system, and some communication gear. Intensive trials and training will precede work ups before each submarine is declared operationally ready and can join the fleet. For *Victoria* this may take up to two years, but the period will shorten for each subsequent boat.

The navy looked at a variety of manning systems for the west coast boat including the American Blue/Gold system and the Australian double crewing of HMAS *Otway*. However, the final decision is to go with one crew per submarine, at least for the foreseeable future.

The Victorias require substantially less maintenance than the old O boats and are compatible with the synchrolift in the dockyard that has been hauling the O boats out of the water for maintenance for thirty years. The Os were docked for three months every eighteen months but the new submarines will go three and a half years between work periods. The alternate Victoria dockings are more extensive and last six months. The Halifax dockyard will conduct these work periods, which will require the west coast boat to rotate, but private industry will undertake the more extensive refits on the east coast. The Victorias' mid-life refits should occur after fifteen years and it is at this stage that the Canadian navy hopes to add the AIP plug, although it has not yet been approved. This project will have to compete with other Department of National Defence projects for funds and priority as the time approaches.

It was not until the Brits decided to stop operating diesel/electric submarines in 1993 that Canada had a realistic chance of saving the Canadian Submarine Service in a climate of financial restraint and disinterest. When the four almost-new British submarines came on the international market suddenly, the Canadian navy knew at first glance that they would fit the bill. Two factors--availability and affordability--made the Upholders undeniably attractive but it was their suitability that really captured the navy.

The Upholders were available--very available. They could be at sea in two years following an extensive reactivation, just when the O boats would be breathing their last gasp. Even if we could have afforded them, brand new submarines would have taken years to reach operational readiness--years the navy did not have. This unique opportunity also presented Canada with a fiscally responsible way of maintaining our submarine capability. With no capital expenditure and the same operational costs as the old boats, the Canadian navy was able to acquire four modern diesel/electric patrol submarines that will last thirty years.

The suitability component of the equation takes longer to explore and can only be tackled after learning the requirements for a new Canadian submarine and about the details of the Upholder class and its competitors.

After the second flirtation with nuclear-powered submarines ended, the navy has had a stated requirement for a proven diesel/electric design of around 2500 tonnes (submerged) with the potential to operate under the ice. They wanted a submarine that was very quiet and had small crews, low detectability, excellent sensors, first-class tactical data-processing equipment, and six torpedo tubes compatible with the Mark 48 torpedoes already in the Canadian inventory. With the distances involved in Canadian submarine operations, the navy considered a minimum range of 10,000 nautical miles essential. Restated in detail in 1993, the navy's specifications for a new submarine included:

- A capability of operating year-round in northern oceans;

- A capability of independent operations in the western Atlantic, eastern Pacific, and eastern Arctic;

- Propulsion systems that would allow them sufficient range to cross the Atlantic;

- A very low indiscretion ratio (detectability);

- An ability to accept an air independent power retrofit;

- A need to be environmentally acceptable to the Canadian public;

- Acoustic signatures on a par with the submarines that would be likely to operate in Canadian ocean areas;

- Good manoeuvrability;

- Weapon and sensor systems capable of detecting, tracking, localizing, and destroying other submarines and surface vessels;

- A self-defence system capable of countering enemy attack;

- An on-board command, control, communication, and computer system capable of integrating the deployed submarine with other national and alliance forces;

- Low personnel requirements consistent with a peacetime three-watch system and allowing a two-watch system in war;

- An ability to carry Special Forces, such as commandos;

- An ability, if the submarine was disabled on the sea bed, to provide deep sea survival and rescue capability to a depth of 180 m; and,

- A standard of habitability as near as possible to that found in other Canadian warships.

So, with this statement of requirement in mind, which submarines did the navy put on the Canadian short-list in 1993? Choices had diminished since the collapse of the Warsaw Pact and since the US and Britain, historically the providers of Canadian boats, had stopped building diesel/electric submarines altogether. Of the boats available, few met Canada's needs and limited budget.

Germany offered three submarines. The 209 class (known as the most popular export submarine in the world) is unsuitable, being too small; the TR1700, could be a strong contender because it is proven, the right size, and operates with a crew of 29; and the new class, the 212, which will have AIP but is not yet fully proven, and will not be available till 2003 at the earliest. The suitable, but very expensive Dutch Walrus class was no longer being built and two other options were not really options at all. Cash-strapped Canada probably could have afforded the used Russian Kilo class submarines but the cost of upgrading to Canadian standards would have been prohibitive. Needless to say, this boat was never considered. Nor must we forget the French offer made a few years back--always keen to compete, they offered Canada a conventional version of their small nuclear-powered Rubis class, but this has never been proven either.

Chile recently bought two of the French/Spanish Scorpene class submarines with AIP for $613 million. Project Ploughshares led the public to believe these submarines were a better buy than the Upholders but they did not meet the Canadian requirements due to size and endurance. The foreign AIP system would also have counted against them, as well as the price.

That left the A471 Kockums design from Sweden, the largest conventional submarine in the world, which the Australians chose as their new Collins class to replace their Oberons. It is already bigger than Canada wants at over 3000 tonnes, and with air-independent power, could reach nearly 4000 tonnes. These submarines carry a complement of forty-two--six officers and thirty-six sailors--and have a range of 11,500 nm at 10 knots and 9000 nm snorkeling, with a top dived speed of 20 knots. At over $780 million each and still climbing, they are also one of the most expensive conventional submarines on the market. A major problem was that all the above submarines, except for the Kilos, would have taken many years to build, years that Canada no longer had, and would have cost over $500 million per copy.

By contrast, the British Upholder class met the Canadian statement of requirement closely. It is a modern, diesel/electric, patrol submarine designed for the rigors of northern ocean operating areas and is proven in the roles Canada requires.

It has a single skin, teardrop hull with a high beam to length ratio, similar to that of SSNs, which provides excellent manoeuvrability, fuel efficiency, and high-submerged speeds. The two decks down below improve habitability for the crew and allow for a larger combat suite than any competitor. Another important feature was the design emphasis on automation that reduces the crew to forty-nine, eighteen less than each O boat carried.

The Upholders were designed in the early 1980s with a mandate to reduce as much emitted noise as possible, to reduce the crew size, and to integrate the navigation, sensors, and communication systems with the fire control and weapons systems. These British requirements led to a great deal of remote control and automation in the new class. The Admiralty commissioned them between 1988 and 1992 and placed them in reserve in 1993.

HMCS Chicoutimi.

Upholders displace 2455 tonnes submerged and are 70 meters (231 feet) long with a hull diameter of 7.6 m (25 feet). The elongated teardrop hull design is based upon that of the British Trafalgar class nuclear-powered patrol submarine and incorporates the most modern acoustic reduction techniques available. There are 66% less through-hull fittings than in earlier designs, thus reducing maintenance and potential problem areas.

The pressure hull is divided into three main watertight compartments. The after compartment contains all the machinery--diesels, air conditioning plant, and electric motor, etc. Beneath the machinery deck and within the pressure hull are fuel, lubricating oil and compensating tanks. In the middle of the compartment is an escape tower which also serves as access, as well as an easily removed shipping opening that allows a complete diesel engine to be taken in and out for maintenance. The midships compartment

A cutaway of the Victoria class submarine, showing the three watertight compartments and all the masts raised.

houses the control room and the CO's quarters on the upper deck, with accommodation and auxiliary machinery spaces below.

Underneath these two decks are fuel, oil, and water tanks and the aft battery. Two hatches provide access--one aft of the fin for general access and another inside the fin for the bridge--and the five-man lockout chamber used by divers when the submarine is submerged. The forward compartment provides the main weapon stowage, handling and discharge equipment on the upper deck, with ratings accommodation and extensive sonar processing equipment on the second deck. Beneath that is the forward battery. This compartment has three hatches: one angled for torpedo loading; one for escape purposes, compatible with a deep submergence rescue vehicle; and one for access. Torpedo handling is fully automated to reduce personnel needs. The torpedo tubes penetrate the forward dome of the pressure hull into the free flooding bow space. Below this is the cylindrical bow sonar, as well as the equipment for the torpedo discharge system. The free flooding structure also contains No. 1 and 2 main ballast tanks.

A single air-cooled GEC twin armature DC electric motor directly drives the single seven-bladed fixed pitch propeller.

The one-man ship control station in the control room of a Victoria class submarine. Behind is the ship control console which provides remote control sand surveillance of the submarine's functions.

(Credit: BAE Systems)

The motor is separated from the diesel generator by a thermal and acoustic bulkhead and can be connected in series or parallel, as can the two batteries, for a wide range of speeds underwater. The system can be operated fully automatically or manually. The high-capacity chloride batteries improve the boats' submerged endurance to 45% more than that of the old Os (80 hours at 4 knots.) and allow short sprints in excess of 20 knots. The two Paxman VALENTA 16 RPA 200S mechanically supercharged diesels are directly connected to very short single-bearing AC generators and provide a maximum of 12 knots when snorkeling. The diesel exhausts are silenced and have surface and snorkel outlets. The engines and generators are carried on resilient mountings to reduce noise and shock. Remote control for most, and surveillance for all, ship and machinery control systems is centralized in the ship control console in the control room and in the motor room. Automatic control can be applied to the boat's attitude control, main propulsion, and battery charging.

A Victoria's engine room, looking forward.
The port side diesel generator can be seen
below the sailor's feet.

(Credit: BAE Systems)

The fin is made of glass reinforced plastic and is a shape that reduces drag. It houses the submarine's masts--periscopes, snort, radar antenna, ESM, and a sonar transducer.

There are six torpedo tubes in the bow which are designed to fire torpedoes, mines, and anti-ship missiles, and twelve reloads can be carried on shock-protected mountings on the upper deck. Fibre optic sensors which provide continuous feed back to the combat system provide data on the state of the tubes and the weapons inside them. In keeping with Canada's tradition, the newly acquired Upholders/Victorias will not carry anti-ship sub-Harpoon missiles or mines. The American Mark 48 ADCAP (advanced capability) torpedoes, worth over $1 million each, are wire-guided weapons measuring nineteen feet long, weighing 3,480 pounds (1,578.5 kg). They can run 50 km at 55 knots, at depths of about 3000feet (915m). Decoys and countermeasure devices can be fired from two submerged signal ejectors.

The Upholders original fire control system will be replaced by the American Singer-Librascope Mark 1 FCS, installed in the Oberons in the mid-80s. The British shore facility Canada is acquiring along with the submarines will enable the software development, systems integration, and training to take place before the Canadianized submarines become operational.

The British boats are very quiet, which makes them outstanding surveillance platforms. The designers have increased the stealth of the Upholders by adding anechoic tiles to the hull, thus reducing the ability of the metal surface to reflect sound waves, as well as decoupling tiles to decrease the radiated noise from inside the hull. The large bow sonar provides both intercept and range data and provides good target discrimination at long range. The Upholders also have three passive ranging flank arrays on each side of the hull, a passive/active ranging system, and have the capability to use the Canadian towed sonar array. There are the traditional, but very sophisticated, search and attack periscopes, the latter being fitted with a low-light TV and thermal imaging capability. Data from all these sensors, as well as radar and electronic surveillance measures (ESM), are fed via a data bus into the action information organization (AIO) and fire control system (FCS). The use of a dual data bus system simplifies integration of equipment when it is changed or upgraded. The Upholders can detect, classify, and track up to thirty-five targets simultaneously.

The Upholders may be the only choice the Canadian navy had but they are not unsuitable simply because there were no viable competitors. They meet the requirements of the Department of National Defence, are proven operationally, and will be able to perform all the roles expected of them well into this century, including Arctic operations later on. With surveillance and control taking priority in the 21st century, their extreme quietness make the Upholders a good choice.

The Canadian navy has said repeatedly in documents obtained through Access to Information that the Upholders are one of the most capable diesel/electric submarines in the world. It also believes the acquisition provides outstanding value for money, given the creative financing package negotiated by DND and the Upholder Sales Team. The only pity is there can be no more than four.

(A table of comparison between the Victoria and Oberon class submarines can be found overleaf.)

PARAMETERS	Victorias	Oberons
Displacement: Surfaced (tonnes) Dived	2,168 2,455	2,030 2,410
Length (feet/meters) Beam	231/70 24/7.4	295/90 25/8.1
Diving depth (feet/meters) Operating depth	600/185 200/60	550/168
Speed: surfaced (knots) dived snorting	12 20 12	12 17 10
Range	8,000 nm @ 8 Kt	9,000 nm @ 12 Kt
Endurance (days)	45	70
Propulsion: shaft x blade, HP main generators main battery	1 x 7, 4000HP 2 x 1400 kW 8800AH	2 x 5, 3500 HP total 2 x 1280 kW 8400AH
Sensors: towed array sonar active/passive sonar sonar intercept ESM/ELINT radar periscope: visual low light IR	Yes Yes/yes Yes Yes/yes Yes Yes Yes Yes	Yes Yes/yes Yes Yes/no Yes Yes Yes No
Torpedoes: Type and load Tubes	Mk 48 Mod 4 (18) 6 forward	Mk 48 Mod 4 (20) 6 forward
Complement	49 (Canadian)	67
Automation	Extensive	Minimal
Acoustic signature	Extremely quiet Anechoic tiling	Fair No tiling

Table 3. A comparison between the Victoria and Oberon submarines

Chapter 15
INTO THE NEW MILLENIUM

As Canadian submariners prepare to accept the Victoria class submarines, they are experiencing new emotions, or at least, emotions some have not felt for decades. Relief at the restoration of a realistic career in submarines; pride in having a modern, suitable class of diesel/electric boats; and excitement at the prospect of serving in a submarine that can operate with the best in the world. They deserve to enjoy these feelings and their new boats.

Canadians should be proud too, though few will pay much attention to the arrival of the Victorias or the work they will do. The new submarines will operate, as before, quietly, with little fuss, and out of the public eye. They probably will not star in movies and will never become the household name that the Snowbirds have. A pity, perhaps, but their invisibility is their strength and something we should preserve for the safety of those who serve in them.

The Upholder acquisition has pleased our allies, especially the US--a stance they rarely take on Canada's defence issues. They see it as evidence that Canada is coming to grips with military deficiencies which have effectively dropped our strength below that which was needed to meet our share of NATO commitments, as well as providing the only diesel/electric submarines in North America--an important bonus for them. The Royal Navy are delighted that the Upholders have gone to a senior ally and sister nation and that they can stop spending $6 million a year on their upkeep.

At home, politicians are either non-committal in public or outspokenly opposed to the new *Victorias*, only the defence minister speaks openly in favour. The federal NDP leader, Alexa McDonough, for example, criticized the acquisition saying, "There are more pressing concerns than the threat of invasion by a foreign enemy"[82] and implied that the money should be spent on more social programs.

Other detractors have cited the age of the Upholder design as being a disadvantage. Certainly it dates back to the early-80s, but so were the other competitors' designs, including the Australian Collins class that some would have us believe is newer. When Canada started looking at diesel/electrics again in 1990, the Collins was still not proven. Perhaps the idea that the submarines are "old" comes from the fact that they are second-hand. The Upholders are actually nearly new and have a thirty-year lifespan ahead of them when Canada takes possession. It is not so much the hull design that counts in submarines, but the equipment it contains that makes a boat modern and sophisticated, and in the Canadian Victorias, is fully suitable for their Canadian roles.

Some amateur commentators in Canada have expressed envy over the Australian example. They see another former colony, with whom we have often compared ourselves, building six big new submarines themselves and developing an independence and self-reliance in submarine technology that we long to have. Not only that, the RAN seems to have the blessing of its politicians. These Canadians feel that if we cannot do the same, at least we could *have* the same if we bought four Collins submarines from Australia. However, approaching $800 million each and still climbing due to significant teething troubles with the combat control system, the Canadian government would certainly never have countenanced it.

The matter of limited endurance is a fair criticism. Most modern diesel/electric submarines have a range of 10,000 nm or more and the Upholders', at 8300 nm, is shorter than most. The plan to convert a water tank to fuel will improve their range but it will still be on the limited side for the huge distances the areas of Canada's maritime responsibility demand. That said, the Victorias are capable of a return trip to European waters, including the Mediterranean, or a one-way trip to Asia without refueling. In other words, they have long enough legs needed to operate in all three of Canadian's oceans and beyond.

Arctic surveillance is one role the Victorias cannot undertake at this time, in any real sense, and it is likely to be at least a decade before they can. Whether this is critical now is moot, given the lack of a serious and direct threat to Canada and our allies. However, the navy does have the prospect of a Canadian-designed and built AIP system becoming available in this century, which can be fitted to the Victorias, and it should have excellent export potential to other nations who operate diesel/electric boats.

The one other serious drawback about this acquisition is that we can never get any more Upholders. Most experts agree the minimum number of submarines for Canada is six, and should we eventually need to acquire more, we will be faced with operating two different classes--always a logistic and training challenge. Four boats cannot give year-round coverage but they can suffice for peacetime, giving two on station with the occasional surge to three. Typically, the four Victorias will give us one operational submarine in the northeast Pacific, responsible for the approaches to the Strait of Juan de Fuca, Queen Charlotte Sound, Dixon Entrance, and the Gulf of Alaska; one in the northwest Atlantic for the Grand Banks, the Flemish Cap, Sable Bank and Georges Bank, the Cabot Strait, the Gulf of St. Lawrence, and the Labrador Sea; and one would be left available for contingencies, which could operate beyond home waters. Occasionally, one boat based in Halifax would be able to patrol the ice-free areas of Davis Strait, around Baffin Bay and the Arctic Archipelago choke points.

One of the greatest benefits of replacing our old Oberon submarines is just that--simple replacement--and not the addition of a new capability to the navy. The Report of the Special Joint Committee on Canada's Defence Policy, which represented the citizenry, recommended replacement because it is always cheaper to maintain a capability than acquire one. Expertise and infrastructure come at great cost in the submarine business, whether it is for refits or operations, personnel training or equipment. But it is the submarine operational skills that are the most perishable--personnel lose their edge in surveillance/ASW surprisingly quickly without continual practice. We need to be very cautious about abandoning these skills--it's all too quick and easy to disband a service in the interests of saving money, but in the long run, it usually means spending more. In other words, it is a false and fleeting economy. Fortunately, for Canada, at least in this round of submarine replacement, common sense prevailed.

Another overwhelming benefit of this acquisition is its price-- bargains come rarely, if ever, in the world of defence procurement. Whatever has been and will be said, there is no doubt the Upholders second-hand status saved the Canadian Submarine Service from extinction--the government would surely never have agreed, in the economic climate of the 1990s, to underwrite the cost of buying new boats off the shelf or building our own at $4 billion plus. Although an excellent case exists for acquiring brand new submarines using the cost-versus-value argument, the negative optics probably would not have been overcome for the politicians. The Upholder/Victoria deal breaks new ground in defence contracting, is innovative and fair, and provides Canadian firms some access to the British defence industry. Jobs have been saved and the economies surrounding three Canadian forces bases will be preserved.

Despite the somewhat limited endurance, the Upholders meet the navy's requirements and are definitely appropriate diesel/electric submarines for Canada. They have a typical submarine lifespan left, a suitability to an AIP retrofit, and if subsequent governments keep them upgraded, they will remain modern and sophisticated surveillance platforms. With the Oberons paid off, the relatively short time Canada will have to wait for the new Victorias to be brought to operational readiness is an added attraction.

During the 1990s, Canada came too close for comfort to losing our submarine capability and the expertise that goes along with it. The abolition lobby was strong, well organized, and very vocal, the citizens couldn't have cared less, and the politicians were preoccupied with national unity and ever mindful of their need for public support. The saviour, if one can be identified, was really two--the sudden availability of four suitable, cheap submarines and the Turbot War. The former provided the navy with a means to acquire new boats at very low cost, thus saving the government from the embarrassment of a huge expenditure, and the latter got the electorate worked up over what they perceived was rightfully theirs. Suddenly Canadians saw a navy which was useful in peacetime and was successfully protecting our sovereignty--fish, in this case.

The four Victoria class submarines at sea.
(Credit: BAE Systems)

One thing is very certain--the long-awaited arrival of the Victoria class will rejuvenate the Canadian Submarine Service not a moment too soon and the navy will gain much more than four submarines. In a maritime nation whose ocean industries are growing in importance and require careful stewardship, they will also restore some of our credibility overseas and will improve our underwater capability sufficiently for the navy to come close to being able to do its job. Although many wags suggested names like *Unmatched, Unbelievable,* and even *Unusual*, the new Canadian submarines will be named after Canadian cities, following the successful example of the frigates.

The arrival of HMCS *Victoria, Windsor, Corner Brook,* and *Chicoutimi* will mark the moment Canadian submarines joined the fleet as full members, participating in the task groups on each coast, and perhaps, overseas too.

They will carry on the tradition of outstanding service to Canada and will preserve and enhance the expertise our submariners have worked so hard to achieve since 1914. The ghosts of Barney Johnson and Willie Maitland-Dougall, are undoubtedly smiling today knowing that their service in Canada's first boats, *CC1* and *CC2,* was not in vain and that the Canadian Submarine Service will continue into the new millennium.

HMCS *Victoria* arrives in Halifax, October 2000
(Credit: Department of National Defence)

Endnotes

[1]. Compton-Hall, Richard. *Submarine versus Submarine.* Newton Abbot, Devon, England: David and Charles Publishers, 1988.

[2]. Ferguson, Julie H. *Through a Canadian Periscope: the Story of the Canadian Submarine Service,* Toronto: Dundurn Press Ltd. 1995; see www.beaconlit.com/beaconli/cdnsubs.html

[3]. The Department of Foreign Affairs and International Trade's website: http://www.dfait-maeci.gc.ca

[4]. Department of National Defence. *1994 Defence White Paper,* Ottawa: Queen's Printer, 1994

[5]. Ibid, 2.

[6]. Thomas, Robert H. "The Canadian Navy: Options for the Future," Canadian Institute for International Peace and Security, Working Paper 41, April 1992, 28.

[7]. For example, CROP and Environics poll, November 1992; and, Pollara poll, February 1997.

[8]. Department of National Defence. *1994 Defence White Paper,* Ottawa: Queen's Printer, 1994, 22.

[9]. Ibid, 28

[10]. Thomas, Charles M.W. "Security Issues Pacific" On *Defence Associations National Network* website: www.sfu.ca/~dann/nn3-6_1.htm, April 1995

[11] Department of National Defence, www.dnd.ca

[12.] Robinson, Bill. "Cuts continue while DND drifts," *Ploughshares Monitor*, March 1996, 9-10.

[13] "Bullet Buying," an editorial. Halifax *Chronicle Herald*, 27 July 199?

[14] Canada 21 Council. *Canada 21: Canada and Common Security in the Twenty-first Century*, Toronto: Centre for International Studies, 1994.

[15] Vice Admiral Peter Cairns, CD, (Ret.)

[16] Gray, Colin S. *Canadians in a Dangerous World,* Toronto: The Atlantic Council of Canada, 1994.

[17.] Special Joint Committee on Canada's Defence Policy. *Security in a Changing World*, Ottawa: Queen's Printer, 1994, 8.

[18] Gray, Colin S. *Canadians in a Dangerous World*, Toronto: The Atlantic Council of Canada, 1994.

[19] Ibid. Much of the previous two paragraphs was taken from *Canadians in a Dangerous World.*

[20] Government of Canada. *1994 Defence White Paper,* Ottawa: Queen's Printer, 1994.

[21] Caldwell, Nathaniel French. *Arctic Leverage:Canadian Sovereignty and Security*, New York: Praeger, 1990.

[22] Crickard, F.W. and Peter Haydon. *Why Canada Needs Maritime Forces,* Ottawa: Napier Publishing Inc. for the Naval Officers Association of Canada, 1994, 5.

[23] Caldwell, Nathaniel French. *Arctic Leverage:Canadian Sovereignty and Security*, New York: Praeger, 1990.

[24] Thomas, Captain (N) Robert H. "The Canadian Navy: Options for the Future," Working Paper 41, Canadian Institute for International Peace and Security, April 1992; and Hill, RAdm JR. *Maritime Strategy for Medium Powers,* Annapolis: Naval Institute Press, 1986, 154

[25] Brodeur, Nigel. "Military Expenditures – Can We Put Them to Better Use?" Previously on *Defence Associations National Network* web site: www.sfu.ca/dann, October 1993.

[26] Ibid.

[27] Brodeur, Nigel. "Defence Spending Constraints and The Federal Debt." Previously on *Defence Associations National Network* web site: www.sfu.ca/dann, October 1993.

[28] Department of National Defence. *1994 Defence White Paper*, Ottawa, Queen's Printer, 1994.

[29] Hill, Radm J.R. *Maritime Strategy for Medium Powers*, Annapolis: Naval Institute Press, 1986.

[30] Bellamy, Christopher. *Knights in White Armour: the New Art of War and Peace*, London: Random House (UK) Ltd., 1996.

[31] VCDS Defence Planning Guidance 2000, www.vcds.dnd.ca/

[32] Thomas, Robert. "The Canadian Navy: Options for the Future," Canadian Institute for International Peace and Security, Working Paper 41, April 1992.

[33] Haydon, Peter. "Sea power in a Changing World." Ottawa: Nepean Publishing Inc. for the Naval Officers' Association of Canada, July 1997.

[34] Ibid

[35] Johnston, Adm. Bruce. "Canada and the Asia Pacific: The Security Link." On *Defence Associations National Network* website: http://www.sfu.ca/~dann/

[36] Minutes of Proceedings and Evidence of the Special Joint Committee of the Senate and House of Commons on Canada's Defence Policy, 31 May 1994, Ottawa: Queen's Printer, 1994.

[37] Osbaldeston, Gordon, F. *All the Ships That Sail: a Study of Canada's Fleets*, 1990

[38] Crickard, Fred W, and Peter T. Haydon. *Why Canada Needs Maritime Forces,* Ottawa: Nepean Publishing Inc. for the Naval Officers' Association of Canada, 1994.

[39] Thomas, Captain Robert H. " The Canadian Navy: Options for the Future," Working Paper 41, the Canadian Institute for International Peace and Security, April 1992, 33.

[40] Ibid

[41] Capt(N) Allan Dunlop,CD (Ret).

[42] Conference of Defence Associations. " Canadian Security: A Force Structure Model for the 21st Century," Ottawa, 1994, 24.

[43] Nesbit, Capt(N) Keith. "Undersea Detection Technology and Naval Arms Control – Some Periscope Views," proceedings of a workshop on the Technology for Arms Control Verification in the 1990s at Ryerson Polytechnical Institute, Toronto, June 1991.

[44] Schwab, Capt. Ernest L., USN (Ret). *Undersea Warriors: Submarines of the World*, Illinois: Publications International Ltd., 1991.

[45] Nesbit, Capt(N) Keith. "Undersea Detection Technology and Naval Arms Control – Some Periscope Views," proceedings of a workshop on the Technology for Arms Control Verification in the 1990s at Ryerson Polytechnical Institute, Toronto, June 1991.

[46] Ibid

[47] Ibid

[48] Maloney, Sean M. "Canadian Subs Protect Fisheries," USNI *Proceedings*, March 1998.

[49] CFN Consultants. " The Potential of a Submarine in Fishery Surveillance and Enforcement, 25 June 1993, obtained through the Access to Information Act; and Maloney, Sean M. "Canadian Subs Protect Fisheries," USNI *Proceedings*, March 1998.

[50] Ferguson, Julie H. *Through a Canadian Periscope: the Story of the Canadian Submarine Service*, Toronto: Dundurn Press Ltd., 1995; see also www.beaconlit.com/beaconli/cdnsubs.html.

[51] Defence Planning Guidance 2000 and Maritime Command Capability Planning Guidance 2000, Department of National Defence, www.dnd.ca, Ottawa, 2000.

[52] Maloney, Sean M. "Canadian Subs Protect Fisheries," USNI *Proceedings*, March 1998.

[53] Ash, James. "Canada considers Britain's sub-stitutes," *King's Journalism Review,* November 18,1997. Previously on University of King's College School of Journalism, Halifax, NS, website: www.journalism.ukings.ns.ca/kjr.

[54] Caldwell, Nathaniel French. *Arctic Leverage: Canadian Sovereignty and Security*, New York: Praeger, 1990.

[55] *Minutes of Proceedings and Evidence of the Special Joint Committee of the Senate and of the House of Commons on Canada's Defence Policy,* Ottawa: Queen's Printer, 1994. (Evidence of Michael Young, 31 May 1994)

[56] King, RAdm Jim. In an interview with the author on 31 January 1997.

[57] Ash, James. "Canada considers Britain's sub-stitutes," *King's Journalism Review,* November 18,1997. Previously on University of King's College School of Journalism, Halifax, NS, website at www.journalism.ukings.ns.ca/kjr/.

[58] Sloyan, Patrick J. "Arctic submarine patrols being phased out," the *Philadelphia Inquirer*, 17 November 1997. On its web site at www.philly.com/newlibrary/, then run a search using key words in

title.

[59] "Don't waste money on submarines," Project Ploughshares, December 1997. On website at www.ploughshares.ca/content/MONITOR/monitor97list.html

[60] *Minutes of Proceedings and Evidence of the Special Joint Committee of the Senate and of the House of Commons on Canada's Defence Policy*, Ottawa: Queen's Printer, 1994. (Evidence of Professor J. Granatstein, 19 April 1994.)

[61] The Report of the Special Joint Committee of the Senate and of the House of Commons on Canada's Defence Policy, 1994.

[62] Ferguson, Julie H. *Through a Canadian Periscope: the Story of the Canadian Submarine Service*, Toronto: Dundurn Press Ltd., 1995; see also www.beaconlit.com/beaconli/cdnsubs.html.

[63] DHIST, Nuclear Propulsion, 6901-50.

[64] Ferguson, Julie H. *Through a Canadian Periscope: The Story of the Canadian Submarine Service*, Toronto: Dundurn Press Ltd., 1995; see also www.beaconlit.com/beaconli/cdnsubs.html.

[65] "Acquisition of Upholder Class Submarines," briefing note for the minister, 10 June 1997. Made available under Access to Information Act.

[66] Ibid.

[67] Department of National Defence website at http://www.dnd.ca, 7 April 1998.

[68] Haydon, Peter. "The Future of the Canadian Navy," *Canadian Defence Quarterly*, December, 1990, 8.

[69] *The Minutes of Proceedings and Evidence of the Special Joint Committee of the Senate and House of Commons on Canada's Defence Policy*, Ottawa: Queen's Printer, 1994.

[70] Thomas, Robert H. "The Canadian Navy: Options for the Future," Canadian Institute for International Peace and Security, Working Paper 41, 47.

[71] Hadley, Michael L., eds., Rob Huebert, and Fred W. Crickard. *A Nation's Navy: In Quest of Canadian Naval Identity*, Montreal and Kingston: McGill-Queen's University Press, 1996.

[72] Ferguson, Julie H. *Through a Canadian Periscope: the Story of the Canadian Submarine Service*, Toronto: Dundurn Press Ltd., 1995; see also www.beaconlit.com/beaconli/cdnsubs.html.

[73] Ibid

[74] "No New Submarines," the *Globe and Mail*, editorial, 13

February 1996.

[75] "Torpedo This Purchase," the *Ottawa Citizen*, editorial, 14 February 1996.

[76] Editorial, *Vancouver Sun,* 17 August 1996

[77] "No subs needed," *Globe and Mail*, 7 April 1998.

[78] "Canada set to buy 4 British subs," *Globe and Mail*, 2 April 1998.

[79] Department of National Defence, *1994 Defence White Paper*, Ottawa: Queen's Printer, 1994s

[80] Upholder Sales Team, at an interview in July 1997.

[81] Cairns, Vice Admiral Peter, CD. Possibly in a speech given in February 1996.

[82] Moore, Charles W. "Canada's new U-boats are the deal of the century, but Alexa and the NDP aren't buying." www.freeyellow.com/members2/barque/uboats

APPENDIX 1

WORLD WIDE INVENTORY OF DIESEL/ELECTRIC SUBMARINES 1998

Statistics can be misleading, especially when it comes to counting submarines. Depending on how one counts, there are 475 conventional--or non-nuclear powered--submarines in the world, including about ninety midget submarines. If this number reflects only those boats that can be classed as truly operational and currently in commission, the total is closer to 450. Even then, some of the inventory is in operational reserve and some of the "midget" submarines can only carry swimmers as their weapon load. Nevertheless, the current total of around 400 is not likely to increase significantly as navies replace old boats on a one-for-one basis.

While the overall number of submarines may drop eventually, what is significant is the quality of the capability that remains. Many navies are now completing, or have completed, upgrading combat and weapons systems in their submarines and so, though the construction date may make the boats seem old, in reality their capability is very much up-to-date.

Note: Figures in bold face indicate theoretically operational submarines. Other figures indicate hulls planned, building, or non-operational status boats.

Also the table above was originally published in the spring 1997 edition of the Naval Officers' Association of Canada's Starshell *and is reproduced here with kind permission. The then editor, Michael Young, compiled it from data in* Jane's Fighting Ships, 1996-97 *and* Jane's Underwater Weapons, 1996-97 *and updated it for the author from* Jane's Fighting Ships, 1999-2000.

COUNTRY	#	CLASS	IN SERVICE	REMARKS
Algeria	2	Russian Kilo	1987-88	Ex-Soviet ROMEO (training)
Argentina	2	German TR 1700	1984	2 others cannabalized for parts
	1	German 209	1974	Modernized 1994-95
Australia	2+4	COLLINS	1996	Problematic combat systems - first truly operational boat 2005.
	1	OBERON	1967-78	Retained for trials and tests. Others scrapped.
Brazil	0+2	TIKUNA (improved TUPI)	2004	Interim step towards SSN
	3+1	TUPI (German 209-1400)	1989-99	
	3	HUMAITA (OBERON)	1973-77	Partially modernized
Bulgaria	3	Russian ROMEO	1972-86	Obsolete; ? operational

Canada	0+4	VICTORIA (British Upholders)	2000-	Being reactivated in UK.
	1+2	OBERON	1965-68	2 paid off in 1998. 1 paid off in July 2000.
	1	OBERON	1989	Used for non-operational harbour training. Incapable of diving.
Chile	0+2	SCORPENE	2004	1st boat building in France
	2	THOMSON (German 209-1300)	1984	Modernized
	2	OBERON	1976	Modernized
China	1	Russian GOLF		Missile trials platform
	1+2	SONG	1994	?MING replacement
	4	Russian KILO	1995-	
	17+2	MING	1971-	
	38+31	Russian ROMEO W	1962-84	Obsolete-31 in reserve; 1 modified SSG
Columbia	2	Type 209-1200	1975	Modernized 1990-91
	2	Midgets	1972	Enlarged in early 80s; carry 8 attack swimmers
Denmark	2	NARHVALEN	1970	Modernized 1990-93
	3	Ex-Norwegian KOBBEN	1986-89	Modernized
Ecuador	0+2+1	GAL (Vickers Type 540)	?	2 and ? a 3rd from Israel
	2	German Type 209-1300	1977-78	Modernized
Egypt	4	Chinese built ROMEO	1982-84	Modernized in US
France	2	AGOSTA	1977-78	Modernized

Germany	0+4 +4	Type 212	2003	1st operational 2003; all with fuel cell AIP
	12	Type 206/206A	1973-75	Modernized.
	2	Type 205	1966-69	Obsolete. For replacement with Type 212
Greece	0+3 +1	HDW Type 214	?	Planned
	4	German Type 209-1200	1979-80	Being modernized
	4	German Type 209-1100	1971-72	Modernized
India	9+1	Russian KILO	1986-97	
	4+2	German Type 209-1500	1986-94	Modernized
	5	Russian FOXTROT	1970-74	Considered obsolete
Indonesia	2	German Type 209-1300	1981	Partially modernized
Iran	3	Russian KILO	1992-97	
	3+?	Midgets	1988-	As many as 9 reported.
Israel	2+1	Type 800 - IKL design	1999-	Similar to Type 212
	3	UK Type 540	1977	Vickers design; modernized; to be sold to Ecuador.
Italy	0+2 +2	Type 212A	2005?	Joint venture with Germany. Fuel cell AIP
	4	Improved SAURO	1988-95	
	4	SAURO	1980-82	
Japan	2+4	OYASHIO	1998-	Improved HARUSHIO
	7	HARUSHIO	1990-97	
	9	YUUSHIO	1980-89	
	1	UZUSHIO	1978	Training boat

Korea - North	22	ROMEO	1973-75	Obsolete
	22+3	SANG-O	1991-	300 tonne submarine (Yugoslav design)
	40	YUGO	1960s-	Yugoslav design
Korea - South	7+2+6	CHANG BOGO (German Type 209-1200)	1993-	Ongoing program
Libya	4	Russian FOXTROT	1976-83	Assessed as non-operational
Netherlands	4	WALRUS	1992-94	
Norway	6	ULA German Type 210	1989-92	
	6	KOBBEN German type 207	1964-67	Modernized 1988-92
Pakistan	1+2	KHALID (AGOSTA 90B)	1999-	Last to have MESMA AIP
	2	French AGOSTA	1979-80	3 new building
	4	French DAPHNE	1969-70	
Peru	6	German Type 209-1200	1975-83	Modernized late 80s
	2	Modified US MACKEREL	1954	Modernized but used for training
Poland	1	Russian KILO	1986	
	2	Russian FOXTROT	1987-88	
Portugal	3	French DAPHNE	1967-69	
Romania	1	Russian KILO	1986	

Russia	0+2 +1	LADA	2001?	Improved KILO
	18	KILO	1980-93	Construction continuing for export only
	6	TANGO	1972-82	Obsolescent
	6	FOXTROT	1958-71	Obsolescent - used for training only in Baltic
	2	PYRANJA	1988-91	250 tonne boats used to carry swimmers
Singapore	0+4	Swedish SJOORMEN	?	To be transferred from Sweden
South Africa	3	French DAPHNE	1970-77	Modernized 1988. New machinery starting 1996. For replacement.
Spain	4	French AGOSTA	1982-86	
	4	French DAPHNE	1973-75	To be replaced
Sweden	3	GOTLAND	1996-	AIP equipped
	4	VASTERGOT LAND	1987-90	
	3	NACKEN	1980-88	Modernized - 1 fitted with closed cycle diesel
		SJOORMEN	1968-69	For Singapore
Syria	3	ROMEO	1986	None been to sea for years.
Taiwan	2	HAI LUNG (Dutch ZWAARDVIS)	1987-88	
	2	US GuppyII	1973	Training boats

Turkey	4+1	PREVEZE (German Type 209-1400)	1994-	3 more planned 2005+
	6	German Type 209-1200	1975-89	
	2	US TANG	1980-83	Loaned and then bought
	3	US GUPPY IIA/III	1970-73	WWII vintage
Ukraine	1(?) +3	FOXTROT	?	From Black Sea fleet
	1	ROMEO	?	
Venezuela	2	German Type 209-1300	1976-77	Modernized 1992-93
Yugoslavia	1+1	SAVA	1978-82	900 tonne coastal boat
	1+1	HEROJ	1968-70	700 tonne coastal boat

APPENDIX 2
SUBMARINE LINE UP: WEST, EAST, AND NON-ALIGNED

COUNTRY	SSBN/ SSB	SSN	PATROL SSK	COASTAL SSC	TOTAL
USA	27/4	84/12	-	-	111/16
OTHER NATO	9/8	18/2	65/16	41/12	133/38
NATO TOTAL	36/12	102/14	65/16	41/12	244/54
RUSSIA	59	108/7	89/5	(13)	269/12
OTHER EX-WP	-	-	7/1	-	7/1
EX-WP TOTAL	59	108/7	96/6	(13)	276/13
NON ALIGNED	2	5/1	203/64	5	215/65
TOTALS	97/12	215/22	364/86	59/12	735/132

(WP denotes former Warsaw Pact. The figure prior to the / denotes operational submarines, and the second shows submarines under construction.)

Source: Jane's Fighting Ships, 1992-93

SELECTED BIBLIOGRAPHY

BOOKS:

Bellamy , Christopher. *Knights in White Armour: the New Art of War and Peace*, London: Random House (UK) Ltd., 1996.

Caldwell, Nathaniel French. *Arctic Leverage: Canadian Sovereignty and Security*, New York: Praeger, 1990.

Compton-Hall, Richard. *Submarine versus Submarine*, Newton Abbott, Devon, England: David and Charles Publishers, 1988.

Crickard, Fred W. and Peter Haydon. *Why Canada Needs Maritime Forces,* Ottawa: Napier Publishing Inc. for the Naval Officers' Association of Canada, 1994.

Ferguson, Julie H. *Through a Canadian Periscope: the Story of the Canadian Submarine Service*, Toronto: Dundurn Press Ltd., 1995.

Gray, Colin S. *Canadians in a Dangerous World,* Toronto: The Atlantic Council of Canada, 1994.

Griffiths, Franklyn. *Strong and Free: Canada and the New Sovereignty*, Toronto: Stoddart Publishing Company Ltd., 1996.

Hadley, Michael L., eds., Rob Huebert, and Fred W. Crickard. *A Nation's Navy: In Quest of Canadian Naval Identity*, Montreal and Kingston: McGill-Queen's University Press, 1996.

Hill, Rear Admiral J.R. *Maritime Strategy for Medium Powers*, Annapolis: Naval Institute Press, 1986.

PAPERS:

Adams, LCdr. M.J. "Fuel Cells and the Navy," *Maritime Engineering Journal*, October 1994, 15-19

Baird, Katherine. " Canadian naval considerations within the context of United States and NATO maritime strategies: policies, problems, and perspectives," *Canadian Defence Quarterly*, December 1992, 13-18.

Breemer, Jan. "Where are the Submarines?" USNI *Proceedings*, January 1993, 37-42.

Brodeur, Vadm Nigel D. "Military Expenditures - Can We Put Them to Better Use?" The Defence Associations National Network's *National Network News,* October 1993.

"Defence Spending Constraints and the Federal Debt." Ibid.

Byers, R.B. "An Independent Maritime Strategy for Canada,"*Canadian Defence Quarterly*, Summer, 1988.

Boyle, Richard, and Waldo Lyon. "Arctic ASW: Have We Lost?" USNI *Proceedings*, June 1998, 31-35.

Canadian Defence Preparedness Association. "The Budget Challenge," the Defence Associations National Network, *National Network News*, winter 1995/96, at http://www.sfu.ca/~dann/nn3-8_1a.htm

Centre for International Studies. *Canada 21:Canada and common security in the twenty-first century,* Toronto: Centre for International Studies, 1994.

Centre quebecois de relations internationales. *Committee of 13: Report on the review of Canadian defence policy,* Quebec: Centre quebecois de relations internationales, Universite Laval, 1994.

CFN Consultants. "The Potential of a Submarine in Fishery Surveillance and Enforcement," June 1993, released by the Department of National Defence under the Access to Information Act.

Conference of Defence Associations, "Canadian Security: A Force Structure Model for the 21st Century." Ottawa, 1994.

Crickard, Radm F.W. "Submarines for Canada-Strategic Implications," Website of the Naval Officers' Association of Canada, http://www.naval.ca, April 1998.

Curtis, Ian. "Submarines and Small Powers Finally Marry," *Defence and Foreign Affairs Strategic Policy*, November-December 1996, 8.

Department of National Defence. *1994 Defence White Paper*, Ottawa: Queen's Printer, 1994

Foxwell, David. "Submarine programs: a sea of uncertainty." *International Defence Review*, June 1992, 513-520.

Friedman, Norman. "Submarines Adapt," USNI *Proceedings*, November 1994, 70-72.

Goode, Captain (N) Anthony J. "Canada: a maritime nation once again?" *Canadian Defence Quarterly*, March 1996, 23-28.

Government of Canada, "Defence Planning Guidance 2000," Ottawa, 1999, .

"Economic and Social Impacts of Submarine Acquisition Options," Ottawa: March 1992.

"Maritime Command Capability Planning Guidance 2000," Ottawa, 1999, www.dnd.ca/navy/marcom.

Maritime Strategy: report of the House of Commons Standing Committee on National Defence and Veterans Affairs, Ottawa, 1990.

Minutes of Proceedings and Evidence of the Special Joint Committee of the Senate and of the House of Commons on Canada's Defence Policy, Ottawa, 1994.

Project Report 598 of Operational Research and Analysis Establishment of the Department of National Defence, "Economic and Social Impacts of Submarine Acquisition Options, Ottawa, 1992.

Report of the Sub-committee on National Defence of the Standing Senate Committee on Foreign Affairs, Ottawa, 1983.

"Security in a Changing World," report of the Special Joint Committee on Canada's Defence Policy, 1994.

"Strategy 2020," Ottawa, 1999, www.vcds.dnd.ca/

"The Maritime Vision: Canada's Maritime Forces in 2015," Ottawa, 1995.

"The Naval Vision: Charting the Course into the 21st Century," Ottawa, 1994.

Griffiths, LCdr D.N. "The maritime face of peacekeeping,"

Canadian Defence Quarterly, September 1995, 12-16.

Griffiths, Rudyard. " New Security Reality," The Defence Associations Network's *National Network News*, volume 4, no. 3, July 1997.

Haydon, Peter. "Our Maritime Future," Naval Officers' Association of Canada, possibly April 1998.

Submarines Make Sense...Far More than the Opposing Rhetoric!" The Defence Associations Network's *National Network News*, volume 4, no. 2, April 1997.

" Sea power in a Changing World," The Defence Associations Network's *National Network News*, volume 4, no. 3, July 1997.

"Implementing the 1994 White Paper. Submarines: the Issues, the Facts, and Some Myths," *Strategic Datalink #50*, Canadian Institute of Strategic Studies, July 1995.

Is Anti-submarine Warfare Dead?" *Canadian Defence Quarterly*, May 1993, 15-23.

The Legacy of the Soviet Navy: Will a Phoenix Rise?" *Canadian Defence Quarterly*, April 1992, 25-32.

Hayles, Cdr. Doug and LCdr Doug McLean. "Why Canada Needs Submarines," *Canadian Defence Quarterly*, Summer 1997.

Hazell, Dr. Paul A. " What's the Future for ASW in NATO?" *Sea Technology,* November 1998, 10-17.

Heemskerk, LCdr. K.A. "Air-independent Propulsion for Submarines: a Canadian Perspective," *Maritime Engineering Journal*, October 1991, 6-14.

Holderness, Cmdre V.F. " Relaunch the Non-Nuclear Boats," USNI *Proceedings,* June 1995, 45-46.

Holt, LCdr Ken. "Submarine Surgery," *Maritime Engineering Journal*, October 1997, 8-13

Huebert, Rob. " Submarines, Canada and the United States," *Strategic Datalink #54*, Canadian Institute of Strategic Studies, May 1996.

Johnsson, Per. "Kockums Submarine Systems: the advantage is air independence," *Maritime Defence*, March 1996, 44.

Johnston, Radm Bruce. " Canada and the Asia Pacific: the Security Link," the Defence Associations National Network's *National Network News*, volume 4, no. 4, Fall 1997.

Lindholm, Lt.Cdr. Sverker. "*Gotland*-Class Submarines--A New Breed," *Sea Technology*, November 1998, 25-31

Lindsey, G.R. "Hunting and Hiding in the Deep Blue Sea," the Defence Associations National Network's *National Network News,* volume 4, no. 2, April 1997.

Lindsey, George, and Gordon Sharpe. "Surveillance over Canada," Canadian Institute for International Peace and Security, Working Paper 31, December 1990.

Lok, Joris Janssen. "Conventional submarines: at the forefront of naval developments, *Jane's Defence 96 The World in Conflict*, 126-131.

Longworth, Brian. " New currents pull undersea warfare," *Jane's Navy International*, May/June 1995, 16-20.

Luttwack, Edward N. "Toward Post-heroic Warfare," *Foreign Affairs*, Volume 74, No. 3, May-June 1995, 109-122

Mainguy, Dan. "Submarines," the Defence Associations National Network's *National Network News,* Volume 3, No. 5, January 1995.

Mason, Radm L.G. "Why Submarines?" *Canadian Defence Quarterly*, June 1992, 21-23.

Moore, Charles W. "Will the Chretien Liberals Blow the Submarine Deal of the Century?" http://www.freeyellow.com, May 1998.

Morton, Desmond. "The NATO Alliance: Do North Americans Care?" The Defence Associations National Network's *National Network News*, Volume 3, No. 6, April 1995.

Nesbit, Capt(N) Keith. " Undersea Detection Technology and Naval Arms Control - Some Periscope Views," *Controlling the Global Arms Threat*, Aurora Papers 12, (proceedings of a workshop on the Technology for Arms Control Verification in the 1990s), Ryerson Polytechnical Institute, Toronto, June 1991.

Newman, Peter C. " The Case for Buying Four British Subs," the Defence Associations National Network's *National Network News, volume 4, No. 4,* Fall 1997.

Reader, G.T. and J.G. Hawley. "Synthetic Atmosphere Diesel Engines for Use in Underwater Vehicles," *Maritime Engineering Journal*, October 1991, 15-20

Robinson, Bill. "Cuts continue while DND drifts," *Ploughshares Monitor*, March 1996, 9-10.

Rosenlof, Cdr Eric. "Contingency Blues," USNI *Proceedings*, January 1995, 53-57.

Sylvestre, Lt (N) Richard. "An Introduction to Stirling Engines and their Use in Submarines," *Maritime Engineering Journal*, April 1988, 8-13.

Thomas, Charles M. W. " Security Issues Pacific," the Defence Associations National Network's *National Network News, volume 3, no. 6,* April 1995.

Thomas, Capt(N) Robert. "The Canadian Navy: Options for the Future," Canadian Institute for International Peace and Security, Working Paper 41, April 1992

Young, Michael. "Hazardous Duty: Nuclear Submarine Accidents," *Starshell*, Fall 1996, 7-10.

"Submarines for the Canadian Maritime Forces," *Canadian Defence Quarterly*, Summer 1986, 25-36.

No author." MARCOM Plots a New Course," *Jane's Navy International*, July/August 1995, 42-48.

No author. "Submarine Modernisation," *Jane's Defence Systems Modernisation*, July 1995, 15-20.

No author. "Submarines: No Rationale," *Ploughshares Monitor*, September 1988, 1-5.

ABOUT THE AUTHOR

Vancouver-based author, freelance writer, and professional speaker, Julie H. Ferguson, has been studying and writing about the Canadian Submarine Service since she visited HMCS Okanagan in 1979. Her first book, *Through a Canadian Periscope: The Story of the Canadian Submarine Service* (Dundurn 1995) was acclaimed as a "major contribution to our naval history" and was selected for *Books for Everyone* at Christmas 1995.

Julie is also an accomplished trainer, leading workshops at writer's conferences and a community college that provide aspiring authors with the insider knowledge, skills, and confidence they need to approach publishers with their work. She is a proud member of the Federation of BC Writers and the Canadian Association of Professional Speakers.

Julie can be reached through info@beaconlit.com or her website at www.beaconlit.com.

IF YOU LIKED *DEEPLY CANADIAN*, ORDER COPIES FOR YOUR FRIENDS AND FAMILY!!

Order from: Phone: (604)469-1319
Fax: (604)469-1316
Email: orders@beaconlit.com
Web: www.booksurge.com or
www.beaconlit.com
Or your favourite bookstore

ISBN: 0-9689857-0-X

Price: $22.99 each (Canadian) + $5.00 shipping

You can also order with a money order for $27.99 from:
Beacon Publishing
#5-300 Maude Road
Port Moody, BC
V3H 2X6
Canada

*****

ALSO TRY JULIE'S FIRST BOOK:

Through A Canadian Periscope: The Story Of The Canadian Submarine Service.
(Dundurn 1995)

Order through your favorite bookstore or from University of
Toronto Press at utbooks@gpu.utcc.utoronto.ca or 1-800-565-9523
ISBN: 1-55002-217-2

64442940R00137

Made in the USA
San Bernardino, CA
22 December 2017